THE COST
OF CAPITAL

Wilbur G. Lewellen

PURDUE UNIVERSITY

THE COST
OF CAPITAL

KENDALL/HUNT PUBLISHING COMPANY

Dubuque, Iowa

Library of Congress Catalog Card Number: 75—35384

ISBN 0—8403—1333—0

Printed in the United States of America

PREFACE

The twin problems of deciding upon the "right" combination of capital sources for a business enterprise, and of determining the cost to the firm of that combination, have occupied the attention of a large number of financial scholars and practitioners during the last two decades. The issues have been confronted from a range of viewpoints—some might say prejudices—which are exceeded only by the variety of the conclusions reached and the list of publications generated. The objective of this book is to draw together and synthesize the threads of those discussions in a way that, hopefully, will provide an integrated view of the corporate financing decision. As such, the book's claim to merit lies less in the fundamental discoveries it makes than in its attempt to make the relevant discoveries comprehensible to the interested reader. It is, in short, intended to be a teaching document.

Throughout the discussion, four themes will be dominant: first, that a firm's basic financial goal should be to maximize the market price of its common stock; second, that the key to this goal lies in developing a coherent model of security valuation; third, that the American capital market is an efficient and rational environment in which security prices equilibrate quickly; and fourth, that the opportunity for individual investors to engage on their own in many of the financial operations which corporations execute must be considered the primary reference point for any meaningful treatment of capital structure decisions. All four propositions would, I believe, be concurred in by the great majority of present-day investigators in the field. The results portrayed in the book follow inevitably from that perspective.

I am greatly indebted to a number of my colleagues at Purdue University and elsewhere for their encouragement in developing the analysis, and for their incisive comments and suggestions. Particular thanks are due Professors Robert Johnson, Gary Schlarbaum, and Gordon Wright of Purdue, Professors Daniel Holland and Stewart Myers of MIT, Professor David Ewert of Georgia State University, Professor George Racette of the University of Oregon, and Professor Paul Cootner of Stanford University. Actually, any errors that remain may be partly their fault as well—though I formally assume that responsibility for myself. Special mention must also be made of the contributions of my secretary at Purdue, Mrs. Yolonda Oswalt, for making it possible finally to get it all down on paper. Her skills in that regard are a continual source of wonder.

WGL

CONTENTS

1

INTRODUCTION

The determination of a business firm's "cost of capital" is one of the most complex and challenging problems in the field of finance. Indeed, if the diversity of viewpoints expressed in the extensive literature on the subject during recent years is taken as a guide, it is also one of the most contentious. The question at issue is simply stated: what is the optimum combination of long-term sources of funds for the profit-seeking enterprise to employ? That it is not so simply answered is primarily a result of the fact that the considerations relevant to its solution involve those features of our economic environment which are most difficult to analyze satisfactorily— namely, the subjective reactions of individual investors to prospective opportunities for profit and the uncertain nature of such prospects in any realistic business situation. The task of the discussion that follows is to attempt to distill from the literature in this area a coherent presentation of the state of the art as it now exists. The ultimate aim, however, is not merely to provide the student of finance with an appreciation of the problems and ambiguities that often frustrate the development of neat solutions, but rather to reach some conclusions that will permit him to function in a business enterprise and make a practical contribution to its success.

ORIENTATION

As the preceding paragraph implies, the concern here is with the long-run operations of the firm and with choices among those funds which support such operations—i.e., the equity investment of the firm's owners and the long-term debt supplied by creditors. The orientation can be described as managerial in that the objective throughout will be to generate a set of criteria for improving the decision-making ability of those individuals charged with the responsibility of running a business. On the other hand, a considerable dose of "theory" as a starting point appears to be the best way to approach this objective, since it simply is not possible to say anything very meaningful about the optimal mix of finance for a corporation without first creating a unified framework of analysis. Fortunately, theory can in this instance bring us quite close to reaching some useful conclusions about practical matters.

One caveat is worth noting at the outset. Those readers who have had some previous experience with the literature on cost of capital will soon detect the fact that into the subsequent chapters have crept the author's value judgments as to which "side" of the continuing controversy in this area offers the more convincing arguments. Because some controversy does exist, it is virtually impossible to attempt to offer a set of guidelines for making decisions without implicitly choosing a particular viewpoint. Attention is paid throughout, however, to both the theoretical and practical objections which may render certain of the conclusions less precise than they at first appear.

THE FINANCE OBJECTIVE

Any discussion of procedures for administering the financial affairs of a business organization must begin by specifying the standard by which the appropriateness of decisions is to be judged. Since the owners of the firm—its shareholders—have put up the funds to establish the business and are the ones who must bear the risks associated with its operations, it seems reasonable that the actions which the financial manager of the firm takes should have as their goal an increase in the material well-being of its owners. The question therefore becomes: What is the proper measure of that well-being?

If we accept the proposition that the aim of an individual's economic activities is to become wealthier, the answer is clear. The most succinct and comprehensive index of a stockholder's wealth is simply the market price of the shares he owns. The higher that price, the bigger an "economic man" he is and the greater is his ability to exercise command over the community's scarce resources. He can sell his shares in order to consume more goods and services and undertake alternative investments on more favorable terms—or he can merely bask in the warm glow of his improved position until such time as he does decide to transform his holdings into cash. Whatever his choice, if wealth is our accepted measure of relative economic circumstances and if the way to make the shareholders of the firm wealthier is to raise the price of their stock, the latter should be the objective of every financial decision. The problem of choosing the most desirable combination of long-term funds for a business firm, then, is that of determining the mix of finance which will maximize the market price of its shares. As we shall see, this objective is equivalent to minimizing the firm's cost of capital.

The difficulties encountered in developing decision rules that will achieve this result are, of course, far from trivial. An obvious and major problem is the fact that stock prices are influenced by a wide range of factors which have nothing to do with a corporation's financing strategies and which are quite beyond its control. The amplitude of the fluctuations in all segments of the stock market over the past few decades—indeed, over the past few years—bears eloquent witness to the strength of these factors. It is necessary, therefore, to sort out in our discussion the impact of financing decisions *per se* and to content ourselves with statements to the effect that "such-and-such a strategy should maximize share price if all other conditions are held constant."

The second problem is methodological. Although our interest is in stock prices, a model of price behavior can be constructed only by examining the nature of the prospective income stream which is associated with the particular share under consideration. Clearly, investors are attracted to or repelled by a company's stock according to their appraisal of the size of the future cash receipts which they can expect from its purchase. In consequence, today's stock price is not a self-contained parameter; it is rather the present value of future receipts as perceived by the prevailing sentiment in the market. The factors which affect price, therefore, are precisely the ones which affect the magnitude and variability of a firm's future earnings. For this reason, our analysis of the desirability of a given financing decision must be cast largely in terms of its impact on the income prospects of the firm's shareholders.[1]

SECURITY VALUATION AND THE COST OF CAPITAL

It should be emphasized from the start that if we adopt the market price of his company's shares as the financial manager's basic decision criterion, his role in executing his responsibilities becomes very much like that of the role of the external security analyst who appraises the

---

[1] The question as to whether investors are primarily interested in a corporation's dividends or its *total* earnings will be considered in some detail later.

firm's operations. The way to increase the price of a corporation's stock is simply to do those things with its finances that will appeal to investors—and, in particular, to those organizations which advise investors. Accordingly, the problem of making an optimal financing decision is the problem of determining how the market will react. Since it is the investment bankers, the stock brokers, and the financial advisory services who provide individual investors with much of their market information, the financial manager must understand and respond to the security valuation techniques these men employ. In that respect, the process of maximizing share price—of minimizing capital cost—is equivalent to the process of security valuation. This link to the attitudes and perceptions of the investment community is the essence of finance, and it will be a cornerstone of our subsequent discussion.

THE PROFESSIONAL MANAGER

One possible objection to the foregoing in connection with actual business situations concerns the reasonableness of expecting a firm's executives to behave as if the welfare of its shareholders were paramount. Is it realistic to believe that executives do—or sensible to suggest in a normative model that they *should*—act in such an altruistic manner? The usual argument against doing so points out that the top executives of most large firms are *professional* managers who receive their rewards in the form of salaries and bonuses rather than as shares in the fruits of ownership. As a result, they are unlikely to be as intimately concerned with stock prices as the discussion above would recommend.

The contention here, however, will be that this apparent separation between ownership and management—and between their respective aspirations—is substantially overstated. Even if it were true that top executives owned no stock in the corporations they manage, they would still have a strong interest in making decisions which would raise share prices, simply because that would be the easiest way to keep their stockholders happy and thereby achieve increases in their own compensation. There are remarkably few instances of shareholder discontent with a management group whose actions have produced a steady increase in the firm's stock price over time.

Apart from this, a more direct relationship between the economic well-being of owners and managers does in fact exist. Even in the largest corporations, top executives are not merely hired hands but are themselves owners of fairly large amounts of the company's stock.

Thus, it is not necessary that a firm's president or financial manager own most of the company himself in order that he behave like a man who really has its shareholders' interests at heart. It is sufficient that he have enough of his personal investment portfolio committed to its stock that an increase or decrease in price has a noticeable impact on his own wealth. The proxy statements issued by publicly held corporations in connection with their annual shareholders' meetings record the stock holdings of top executives. A quick glance at these statements reveals that investments of several hundred thousand dollars by senior officers are not uncommon. Under such circumstances, it is reasonable to assume that executives are sensitive to share prices.

Further support for this belief comes from an examination of the nature of the present-day executive compensation "package." Because our federal income tax laws have made it advantageous for corporations to reward their highly paid employees by means other than the traditional salary and bonus payments, various deferred and contingent compensation arrangements have increased markedly in importance over the last quarter century. In recent years, from one-third to one-half the total after-tax remuneration of top corporate executives has been provided by devices—such as stock options—which in one form or another utilize their firms' common stock as the compensation medium.[2] An ownership-oriented attitude among management seems a likely result.

SMALL ENTERPRISES

While an increased share price is *the* mechanism for benefiting the stockholders of a large firm—since that is effectively the only way they participate in its success—the same is not necessarily true in the case of a small, closely held business. There are a wide range of noneconomic satisfactions which the latter's owner-managers derive from its operations, and their main concern may well be with factors other than market values. In addition, of course, there simply may not be a meaningful market for the relevant shares. This suggests that the analysis here is perhaps most applicable to those organizations which are large enough to enjoy a fairly broad public stock distribution and whose shares are traded frequently enough that a

[2] Wilbur G. Lewellen, *Executive Compensation in Large Industrial Corporations* (New York: National Bureau of Economic Research, 1968). . . . W.G. Lewellen, "Managerial Pay and the Tax Changes of the 1960s." *National Tax Journal*, June 1972.

continuing market reaction to management's activities can be obtained. This is not to say that the decision framework to be developed cannot, with certain modifications, be applied to small businesses.[3] The point is instead that the small businessman may have his own set of values that only partially reflect economic objectives. Because he must answer for his actions only to himself, he may legitimately run his business according to his personal tastes. We do not offer the same option to the professional financial manager.[4]

CAPITAL BUDGETING AND THE COST OF CAPITAL

The chapters that follow will deal almost exclusively with managerial decisions relating to the right-hand side of a corporation's balance sheet. To a large extent, this is an artificial restriction and is defensible only in terms of keeping the subject matter of the analysis within reasonable bounds. The asset investments which comprise the left-hand side of the ledger—and which are nominally the province of a capital budgeting treatise—clearly influence the firm's ability to choose among different sources of funds. Because this interdependence between the investment and financing decisions is, after all, the rationale for being concerned with cost of capital calculations, the relationship bears emphasizing before we proceed further.

The object of undertaking a business venture is not merely to earn a return; it is to earn a return *in excess* of the costs associated with the resources employed. Among those resources are the funds which owners and creditors supply. A firm's so-called "cost of capital" then —commonly expressed as an annual percentage figure—is simply that rate of return which its assets must produce in order to justify raising the funds to acquire them. In this light, the tasks of the financial manager which we shall consider here may be regarded as twofold: to provide a required rate of return standard—a cost figure —which the firm can use in appraising prospective investment opportunities;[5] and to arrange its finances in such a way as to minimize that

---

[3] And it should be if the small firm is at all interested in appealing to outside investors or in becoming a candidate for merger or eventual purchase by a larger company.

[4] A discussion of the financial problems of small business is contained in Roland I. Robinson, *Financing the Dynamic Small Firm* (Belmont, Calif.: Wadsworth Publishing Company, Inc., 1966).

[5] For purposes of calculating the present value of those opportunities, for example.

cost. The corporation thereby is, on the one hand, given a criterion for identifying suitable investments and, on the other, is enabled to obtain from them the maximum possible benefit for the shareholders in the form of an increased stock price. Our discussion will cover the issues relevant to both objectives.[6]

ORGANIZATION OF THE BOOK

Since some degree of uncertainty about future returns is a characteristic of almost every business situation, the analysis will begin by exploring the nature of investors' reactions to probabilistic investment outcomes. With that as a foundation, the relative cost of debt and equity funds will be determined—first in an economic environment without personal or corporate income taxes and then under more realistic conditions. Following this, the cost of retained earnings and the question of a corporation's dividend policy will be considered. Finally, the various decision rules will be combined into a "weighted average" cost of capital calculation and that framework applied to a hypothetical corporation in order to illustrate how the numbers might be obtained in practice. The procedure throughout will be to start with a fairly simple model of the problem at issue and then to make it progressively more complex. Hopefully, we shall end up with some reasonably concrete recommendations for the financial manager.

[6] A full treatment of the capital budgeting problem is contained in Robert W. Johnson, *Capital Budgeting* (Belmont, Calif.: Wadsworth Publishing Company, Inc.).

2

UTILITY AND RISK

AVERSION

As indicated in the preceding chapter, our prime concern in making financial decisions should be with their impact on our firm's stock price. Since that price is determined by the transactions undertaken by the multitude of individual investors who comprise the market for securities, the foundation of our analysis must be an appreciation of the preferences and economic objectives of those investors. In particular, it is necessary that we develop some means of taking into account the fact that, while they are attracted by an opportunity for profit, they are likely to react adversely to the risks associated with that opportunity.

THE UTILITY FUNCTION

A convenient vehicle for examining the nature of their attitudes is what an economist would term a "utility function." This is simply a representation of the satisfaction which investors can be thought of as deriving from different amounts of wealth. Although it could be described in mathematical terms, the graphical representation shown in Figure 2–1 will suffice for our purposes here. The various levels of wealth, in dollars, that an individual might conceivably experience are plotted on the horizontal axis and the enjoyment—the inner glow—he would feel at each level is plotted on the vertical scale.

Lest all this seem just too absurd, a few comments are appropriate. First, the curve is an abstraction which should not be taken too literally. It would be very difficult to actually measure the enjoyment or satisfaction felt by an investor in terms that could be made meaningful to someone else. Thus, what would the unit of measure be? "Goods," "wonderfuls," or perhaps "delightfuls"? And what would they mean to an outsider? How many of your "wonderfuls" equals one of my "delightfuls"? Are you as happy with $10,000 in the bank as I am? As we shall see, however, we need not have an *absolute* scale for utility that applies to every investor in order to draw some useful conclusions about risk aversion and its financial implications. It is sufficient that we be able to make statements about the *relative* benefits a *single* individual obtains from successively larger amounts of wealth.

A second issue is that obviously wealth in and of itself does not make people happy—except for a few pathological cases, one supposes

FIGURE 2–1. *An investor's utility function.*

—but rather what wealth can buy. The vertical axis therefore is meant to record the enjoyment an investor would derive from the goods and services which the different levels of wealth shown would permit him to consume. In this respect, wealth is only a proxy measure of his capacity for these other activities, and we must keep in mind throughout our discussion that our investor's interest really is in that second car, that summer home, that trip to Europe—or that large inheritance he intends to pass on to his sons—which an increased stock price can provide.

THE SHAPE OF THE CURVE

Despite its necessarily abstract nature, the utility function pictured above was not chosen at random. The fact that the curve, while steadily rising, falls away to the right at higher and higher levels of wealth[1] conveys two important—and by now reasonably well accepted

---

[1] Or, to be more elegant, the curve is shown to be concave to the origin.

—features of the typical investor's attitudes: (1) the more money he has, the happier he is; (2) but equal successive increments to his wealth imply progressively *smaller* increments to his total utility.

The first of these is perhaps the easier to accept, at least insofar as our objectives here are concerned. This is a business text rather than a philosophical essay. Since in the business world, people attempt to make money, little more need be said to justify a rising utility function. Actually, the arguments to be made below do not require that the curve continually rise—just that it never turn downward. As long as additional wealth is no *dis*advantage to the investor, this will be a legitimate assumption.

The other point—i.e., that the curve is in fact a curve rather than a straight line—may have less logical appeal. As it turns out, this is merely an expression of the familiar economic principle of diminishing marginal returns. An individual eventually becomes somewhat satiated with his wealth. The second million he acquires, while still worth having, is not quite as valuable to him as the first million, since the latter has already provided him with most of the material satisfactions he wanted out of life. Three summer homes do not really generate half again the happiness of two.

We need not, of course, deal with such large sums in order to observe this phenomenon. An income of $20,000 annually is not likely to be twice as desirable as one of $10,000. With the smaller amount, we are already able to move our family out of that crowded in-town apartment to the fresh air of the suburbs, whereas the additional $10,000 simply provides the pine-paneled basement and the color television set that we could have been reasonably happy without. Or, at a still more poignant level, the first thousand dollars we earn permits us to consume enough food at least to stay alive. The second thousand only permits us to have meat more often.

If such intuitive arguments are not wholly convincing, there is considerable empirical evidence to support them. Our discussion is leading up to the conclusion that a utility function of the type illustrated implies that investors dislike risk—and we have clear indications of risk aversion in the real world. We observe that people buy insurance; we see that they diversify their investment portfolios instead of putting all their funds into a single stock; we notice businessmen requiring larger prospective returns from ventures that are highly uncertain than they do from safer investments; and we see corporate bonds rated as grade "B" in terms of the ability of the issuer to meet the required payments selling at a lower price than those rated "Aaa."

Thus, visible economic behavior is consistent with aversion to risk on the part of investors—and our curve, as we shall see, provides the underlying rationale for just such an attitude. In that respect, it is offered here as a rough, but valid, approximation of the wealth-utility responses of most security purchasers.

A final note. The curve is shown to intersect the vertical axis rather than pass through the origin of the graph. For the same reason that the units in which "utility" is measured are arbitrary—indeed, they are irrelevant—so is it a matter of choice as to whether we define a "zero" utility point. The shape of the curve, not its height, is our concern.

RISK AND RETURN

Using this framework, then, let us examine the manner in which an individual would appraise the attractiveness of an investment opportunity whose outcome is uncertain. Since any such investment is basically a form of gambling, we may cast our analysis in a simple betting context for purposes of illustration. Consider the following circumstance: An individual whose total wealth amounts to $1,000 is offered the chance to bet $100 on the outcome of a coin toss. If the coin comes up heads, he wins $100; if it shows tails, he loses $100. The coin is "fair" so that the probabilities of winning and losing are both equal to one-half. The question therefore is: Will this be an attractive proposition?

We can answer that question by looking at his utility function in the region of $1,000 initial wealth. He perceives the possible results of the bet to be as shown in Figure 2–2. At the moment, he has a

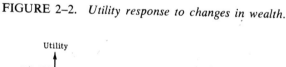

FIGURE 2–2. *Utility response to changes in wealth.*

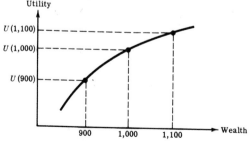

thousand dollars and enjoys the level of satisfaction denoted by $U(1,000)$. That is, the goods and services he could purchase with those funds would provide him with that much "utility." If he accepts the bet and wins, his wealth rises to $1,100 and his satisfaction to $U(1,100)$. If he loses, his wealth declines to $900 and his satisfaction to $U(900)$. Should he gamble?

The answer clearly is no. Although the bet is fair in money terms, it is not fair with respect to what the money means to him. The additional satisfaction he would obtain by winning—the difference between $U(1,100)$ and $U(1,000)$—is less than the pain he would be subjected to in losing—the difference between $U(1,000)$ and $U(900)$. He will bet only if the amount he stands to win is sufficiently greater than his possible loss that the two increments on the *utility* scale are equal, as illustrated in Figure 2–3, where:

$$U(1,130) - U(1,000) = U(1,000) - U(930). \qquad (2\text{–}1)$$

A coin toss having the following outcomes *would* be acceptable: heads, he wins $130; tails, he loses $70. That situation could be achieved by making it a condition of the bet that the other party first pay our man $30 and then flip the coin. In this light, $30 can be

FIGURE 2–3.   *An acceptable bet.*

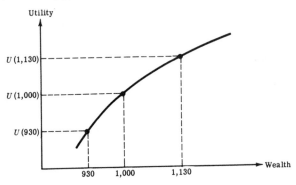

interpreted as the "risk premium" necessary to induce participation. It measures the monetary equivalent of our investor's "risk aversion" to the indicated set of uncertain outcomes.

AN ILLUSTRATION

A concrete example may serve to drive the point home. In the author's student days, he once attended a course in "Managerial

Decision Theory" in which the instructor began the semester by discussing utility functions. On the second day of class, he told us each to come to the next session with $2 in cash—and our check-books. At the beginning of the period, he collected the $2 which, since there were fifty of us in the course, made a "pot" of $100. He then said we were going to be allowed to bid for the right to flip a coin with him for the pot. We were to submit sealed bids, the highest bidder being awarded the chance to flip the coin and either take home the $100 or get nothing. If the student lost, the money was to go to the university's alumni fund. The catch was that first the high bidder had to write out a check for the amount of his bid. That sum also was to go to the alumni fund so that, whatever happened with the coin toss, the bid was gone forever.

The question for us, then, was: How badly did we want to play the game? Its "expected value"—i.e., the average of its outcomes weighted by their respective probabilities—was $50, but a participant would not get $50. He would get either $100 or nothing. Was such a gamble—an investment opportunity, if you will—worth paying $50 to undertake? Those of us who did not want to risk losing anything at all had only to submit a bid of zero in order to effectively opt out of the game. On the other hand, the chance of winning the $100 piled up on the table in the front of the room was not unattractive, and therefore we had some incentive to submit a realistic offer.

Intuition—and the arguments made above—would suggest that a high bid of $50 was unlikely. In fact, the top figure was $35. We would say that, to the student who offered this sum, the gain in satisfaction associated with winning $65—the difference between the $100 pot and his $35 bid—was equal to the unhappiness associated with losing the $35. He had therefore designed a fair game in utility terms. Put another way, his risk premium came to $15—the difference between the game's expected monetary value and his bid. This in effect was the amount the rest of the class paid him to play the game.[2]

DISPERSION AND RISK PREMIUMS

If all this seems reasonable in the context of a single gamble, what can our utility function tell us about the relative attractiveness of different bets? Let us suppose our man with $1,000 is confronted with an additional opportunity. Someone else offers him a heads-or-tails

[2] Actually, we paid him more than that. He won.

FIGURE 2–4.   *Comparison of two gambles.*

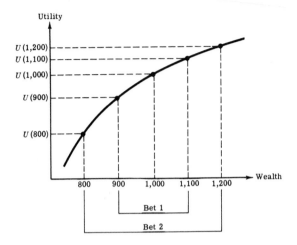

bet in which the stakes now are $200 instead of only $100. We may characterize his reactions by Figure 2–4. If he accepts the first bet, the difference between the utility he stands to gain and that which he stands to lose is

$$\Delta U_1 = [U(1,100) - U(1,000)] - [U(1,000) - U(900)]. \quad (2\text{–}2)$$

In the case of the second bet:

$$\Delta U_2 = [U(1,200) - U(1,000)] - [U(1,000) - U(800)]. \quad (2\text{–}3)$$

Both of which, of course, are negative. By the nature of the curve, however, it will always be true that ΔU_2 exceeds (is more negative than) ΔU_1. The larger the bet—the greater the spread of its possible outcomes for a given monetary expected value—the less attractive it is.[3] An investor therefore must not only be "paid" something to take an even bet; he must be paid more the wider its range of consequences. Thus, he would be indifferent between the two bets if the terms were as in Figure 2–5, where the stipulation is that

$$U(1,130) - U(1,000) = U(1,000) - U(930) \quad (2\text{–}4)$$
$$U(1,250) - U(1,000) = U(1,000) - U(850). \quad (2\text{–}5)$$

---

[3] Put differently, the greater the spread of the dollar outcomes, the more negative is the expected *utility* value of the bet. Implicit in our discussion is the proposition that a "fair" gamble is one with an expected value of zero in utility terms.

FIGURE 2–5. *Comparison of two acceptable bets.*

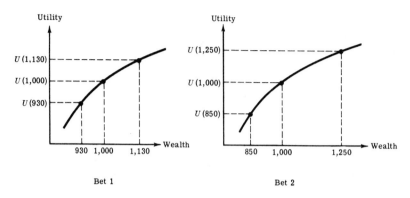

His companions would have to pay him $30 to get him to take number 1, but $50 to take number 2 with its higher stakes. In order to analyze the relative attractiveness of different investments, then, we must recognize not only the expected value of their outcomes but also the relative *dispersion* of the probability distribution associated with each. Fortunately, there is a convenient mathematical measure of that dispersion which we can make use of in our subsequent discussions of alternative financing decisions under uncertainty.[4]

WHY GAMBLE AND INVEST?

The objection might be raised at this point that something must be wrong with the preceding arguments, since they in effect imply that no one in the community would ever either gamble or invest. How can the existence of both activities be explained if we are really to believe that utility functions of the sort described adequately depict individual attitudes?

Take gambling first—in particular, the penny-ante poker game or similar small-stakes endeavors. We can fit these into our mold with only a minor stretching of the analysis. The rationale would be that

---

[4] The terms "risk" and "uncertainty" are being used interchangeably here. Decision theorists, however, would draw a distinction between the two based on the amount of information available about the relevant probability distributions of outcomes. The nature of our objectives does not require that we make that distinction, but the reader may come across it elsewhere in the literature. See, for example, R. D. Luce and H. Raiffa, *Games and Decisions* (New York: John Wiley & Sons, Inc., 1957), p. 13.

the range of possible dollar wins and losses is so small in relation to the players' total wealth that they simply are not sufficiently sensitive to the utility implications to react adversely. The difference between the gain in utility from winning, say, $5 if you have a good night with the cards and the utility loss implied by ending up $5 in the hole on a bad night is just not great enough to notice, much less worry about. If you feel you are as likely to win as to lose such an amount—i.e., you play poker as well as anyone else in the game—you will play despite the minor utility consequences. Few of us, however, will stay in the game when the pots reach $500 per hand. By that time, the happiness connected with winning and the pain produced by losing are far enough out of balance that we abstain. The same phenomenon, of course, is observed where investments in common stocks are concerned. Most people are willing to put only a portion of their total wealth into equities, keeping some of their funds in savings accounts or similar secure investments.[5]

Another reason for gambling is that the process itself has some "utility." It's fun to get together with the boys and match wits. Poker is only the excuse for doing so. If you happen to lose a few dollars every once in a while, you regard that as merely the price of an evening's entertainment. Perhaps a better reason, however, is that you may in fact believe that your chances of winning are better than your chances of losing. You have faith in your ability at cards. You perceive yourself in the situation depicted in Figure 2–3 above where the potential win is $130 while the loss is only $70, so that in utility terms the gamble *is* sensible. This may be the attitude of most so-called "professional" gamblers. They think they know something that their adversaries do not and therefore are willing to participate in the game.[6]

The same reasoning can be extended to investing. The expectation of the investor is that, on average, there *is* an opportunity to profit. The "bet" is weighted in his favor—its expected monetary value is positive. Empirical evidence, of course, supports that attitude. People

[5] This continuing analogy between investing and gambling may not be entirely appreciated by the investment community. The following quotation attributed to the Dallas *Times-Herald* may be pertinent: "If you bet on a horse, that's gambling. If you bet you can make three spades, that's entertainment. If you bet AT&T will go up three points, that's business. See the difference?"

[6] The case of the "compulsive" gambler can also be explained this way. He not only thinks he can come out ahead, but is so enamored of the gambling process that he ignores its possible unhappy results.

do make money in the market if for no other reason than the fact that most firms whose shares are traded are themselves earning a profit from operations. Stock prices seem to be generally rising over time and, while the risks we are concerned with here are clearly present, so are attractive opportunities. The question for us, then, is the manner in which these two aspects of an investment are balanced in an investor's mind.

EXPECTED VALUE AND VARIANCE

The utility function approach described above suggests that the answer lies in an examination of the two features of the probability distribution of investment outcomes which measure "return" and "risk"—the expected monetary value of the investment and its degree of dispersion. The former, as was indicated, is defined simply as the average outcome of the opportunity: the sum of each possible result weighted by its probability of occurrence. Thus, an investment whose characteristics are as shown below has an expected value equal to $1,000.

Possible Outcome, x	Probability of Occurrence, $Pr(x)$	$x \cdot Pr(x)$
$ 900	$\frac{1}{4}$	$ 225
1,000	$\frac{1}{2}$	500
1,100	$\frac{1}{4}$	275
		$1,000

This parameter, which is commonly called the "mean" of the distribution, will hereafter be denoted either by the symbol μ or by a bar over the pertinent variable, e.g., $\bar{x}$.

Similarly, the extent of the possible spread of a set of such outcomes is measured by a parameter termed its "variance" and defined as the squared sum of the deviations from the mean, also weighted by their respective probabilities:

Possible x	$Pr(x)$	$x - \bar{x}$	$(x-\bar{x})^2$	$[Pr(x)][(x-\bar{x})^2]$
$ 900	$\frac{1}{4}$	-100	10,000	2,500
1,000	$\frac{1}{2}$	0	0	0
1,100	$\frac{1}{4}$	$+100$	10,000	2,500
			Variance =	5,000

The greater the potential variation in the results, the larger will be this parameter. Squaring any negative deviations ensures that relationship.

Since variance is usually denoted by the symbol σ^2, we will adopt that terminology.

The point of calculating the variance, it should be emphasized, is that the typical investor's utility function tells us that the greater the range of the consequences of a gamble, the less attractive it becomes. The utility disadvantages of the losses become progressively more severe in relation to the benefits of the profits. For that reason, variance is a convenient proxy measure of the size of the relevant "risk premiums."[7] In the chapters that follow, therefore, a firm's financing decisions will be examined according to their impact on the mean and the variance of its shareholders' prospective income streams, the argument being that these two items tell us essentially all we need to know about their reactions under uncertainty.

[7] To be completely correct, it should be stated that the variance of a set of uncertain outcomes is really only *one* measure of risk insofar as investors' utility perceptions are concerned. Depending on the precise mathematical form hypothesized for the utility function, other higher-order parameters of the various probability distributions may also be of interest. Since variance will always be pertinent, however—and since it is likely to be the most significant risk measure in all cases—we need not inquire about those others for our current analysis. Readers who are familiar with utility function properties will observe that the arguments to be made below could easily be extended to include higher-order factors if desired.

3

THE DEBT-EQUITY
CHOICE: NO TAXES

Let us consider, then, how the preceding analysis can be applied to a corporation's choice of its proper mix of long-term debt and equity funds. To date, the most comprehensive treatment of this problem has been provided by Modigliani and Miller, who conclude that, were it not for the federal corporate income tax, the debt-equity ratio of a firm would have no effect on either its common stock price or its cost of capital.[1] The discussion here will generally parallel their analysis and will begin with the no-tax situation in order to underline the nature of the relevant methodological approach. Taxes will be introduced in Chapter 4.

PHILOSOPHY

The Modigliani-Miller argument is based on the reasonable proposition that identical income streams should not sell for different prices at the same time in a rational securities market. They ask the question: Is it possible for an individual investor, by borrowing on his own and purchasing shares in firms which have no debt in their capital structure, to duplicate the income stream generated by firms that do have debt? If the answer is affirmative, as it is in the absence of taxes, the common stock of "levered" firms[2] cannot command a higher price —and those firms cannot have a lower cost of capital—than ones completely equity-financed.

---

[1] Franco Modigliani and Merton Miller, "The Cost of Capital, Corporate Finance, and the Theory of Investment," *American Economic Review,* June 1958, pp. 261–297, and "Corporate Income Taxes and the Cost of Capital: A Correction," *American Economic Review,* June 1963, pp. 433–443.

[2] The term "levered firm" will be used here to denote any corporation which has some long-term debt on its balance sheet.

THE ANALYTICAL FRAMEWORK

To be more specific, consider two firms in the same line of business. Since they sell to the same group of customers and must buy raw materials from the same range of suppliers, their respective asset investments will give rise to prospective income streams with quite similar characteristics. In this sense, we may define them to be in the same "risk class." For convenience—and because it does not affect the conclusions to be drawn from our analysis—let us further assume the two firms to be of exactly the same size.[3] We therefore may say that, if the actual profits to be earned by each firm in every subsequent year are thought of as being drawn from a probability distribution of possible outcomes for that year, the two corporations can look forward to a sequence of results which have identical means and variances. Finally, in order to defer to a later chapter the problem of dividend policy and growth, let us assume that both companies pay out all their earnings to their stockholders as dividends. They simply reinvest their depreciation allowances to replace worn-out equipment and thereby stay the same size over time.[4]

SHAREHOLDERS' INCOME EXPECTATIONS

If both corporations initially are entirely equity-financed, the total market value of each firm's common stock may be expressed as

$$V = \frac{\overline{Y}}{\alpha}, \tag{3-1}$$

where V is that total market value, $\overline{Y}$ is the mean of the probability distribution of their respective total earnings (and, of course, their total dividends) each year, and α is the discount rate which the investing public uses to appraise the future prospects of companies in this risk class. Thus, the price of a share of stock is nothing more than the present value of the cash flows which investors expect to obtain from owning it. If investors discount a *level* expected income stream at an annual percentage rate, α, the general formula for present value

---

[3] The only effect of this is to remove a scale factor from the subsequent comparisons which has no influence on their validity.

[4] While this clearly represents a somewhat contrived example, it is not an unreasonable or unnecessarily restrictive one. The only objective is to cast the problem in a way which eliminates as many factors as possible that are not directly related to the immediate debt-equity choice.

$$PV = \sum_{t=1}^{\infty} \frac{\overline{Y}_t}{(1 + \alpha)^t} \qquad (3\text{--}2)$$

becomes just

$$PV = \frac{\overline{Y}}{\alpha}, \qquad (3\text{--}3)$$

since all the $\overline{Y}_t$ values are the same and are equal to our $\overline{Y}$, and since the geometric progression

$$\sum_{t=1}^{\infty} \frac{1}{(1 + \alpha)^t} \qquad (3\text{--}4)$$

reduces to simply $1/\alpha$. We are discounting, at least nominally, to "infinity" in this case on the assumption that a corporation is a perpetual enterprise which is expected to remain in operation forever —or, in any event, for as long as we care to think about.

Actually, we do not need to be able to observe the discount rate α directly. We can infer it from the other parameters which we *are* able to observe. Thus, on a per-share basis, we have

$$\frac{V}{N} = P = \frac{\overline{Y}/N}{\alpha}, \qquad (3\text{--}5)$$

where N denotes the number of shares of common stock outstanding for each firm, P their per-share market prices (both the same if N is the same for both), and $\overline{Y}/N$ their expected earnings per share. We can find P in our morning *Wall Street Journal*. We have a good estimate of $\overline{Y}/N$. Therefore, α can be calculated. In fact, the ratio

$$\alpha = \frac{\overline{Y}/N}{P} \qquad (3\text{--}6)$$

is just an "earnings-price" ratio—the reciprocal of the "price-earnings" ratio about which we hear so much in the business press. Because, for the moment, all earnings are being paid out as dividends by both firms, α is also the "dividend-price" ratio, or the so-called "dividend yield."

All we have said so far, then, is that the stock of two firms of the same size in the same line of business which have the same number of shares outstanding and are both completely equity-financed should sell at the same price because the cash income prospects of both sets of shareholders are identical. That hardly seems a surprising conclusion and is worth pointing out only as a basis for what follows.

CORPORATE LEVERAGE

Suppose, now, that one of the two corporations—call it firm A—decides that it really ought to take advantage of the opportunity to employ some borrowed funds instead of relying entirely on shareholders' capital. It decides to issue debt in the amount D for which it must pay interest at an annual rate r to its creditors. It uses the funds thus obtained to retire a portion of its common stock by simply buying back those shares at the price P in the market.[5] The process is set up in this way only to maintain a convenient comparison between the two firms. As an alternative, we could think of firm A using the borrowed funds to undertake new investments and thereby become larger. Since this would, however, re-introduce that scale factor we are trying to eliminate, it seems a less efficient approach.

After the indicated transaction, there will be $N[1-(D/V)]$ shares of firm A's stock still outstanding, the fraction D/V having been retired. That is, D/P shares will have been purchased and we know from above that $P = V/N$. This means that the expected annual earnings —and dividends—associated with each of the remaining shares will be

$$\bar{y}_A = \frac{\overline{Y} - rD}{N\left(1 - \dfrac{D}{V}\right)}, \qquad (3\text{--}7)$$

$\bar{y}_A$ being used to denote now the *per-share* expectations of the firm's stockholders. There are $N[1-(D/V)]$ of them left, but the company can promise them only the annual amount $(\overline{Y} - rD)$ since the portion rD of total earnings must be paid to creditors.

If this is the expression for per-share earnings, and the variance of *total* earnings is denoted by $\sigma^2(Y)$, the per-share variance becomes

$$\sigma^2(y_A) = \frac{\sigma^2(Y)}{N^2\left(1 - \dfrac{D}{V}\right)^2}. \qquad (3\text{--}8)$$

Because we know from the theory of probability that if

$$y = aY, \qquad (3\text{--}9)$$

where a is a constant, then:

---

[5] Which it can easily do. Indeed, many corporations do just that as a matter of continuing policy with their excess cash.

$$\sigma^2(y) = a^2[\sigma^2(Y)]. \tag{3-10}$$

In equation (3–7), the items r, D, N, and V are in fact constants; hence equation (3–8). Since there is no variability associated with the term rD in the numerator of equation (3–7)—i.e., the interest charges on the debt *must* be paid every year—that term drops out of equation (3–8) also. The mathematics of this argument should not be allowed to obscure its content, however. We are simply attempting to isolate the impact of leverage by examining its consequences in terms of the two parameters of the probability distribution of shareholders' future incomes that our utility-of-wealth model in Chapter 2 showed us to be relevant. In order to accomplish this, it is necessary that we translate the mean and variance of *aggregate* corporate profits into per-share magnitudes. The formulation above does nothing more than that.[6]

PERSONAL LEVERAGE

Given the two features, $\bar{y}_A$ and $\sigma^2(y_A)$, of the probability distribution of earnings and dividends associated with each of the now-levered firm A's shares, the question is whether the price of those shares should be expected to rise in response to the firm's new capital structure. Will a levered corporation's stock command a premium in the market over that of another firm—such as our second firm B—which does not employ debt financing but which is in all other respects identical?

In order to answer this question, we should determine whether there is anything unique about firm A's new income stream. Is it possible that an individual investor might obtain the same result for himself by borrowing on personal account and using the borrowed funds to buy into firm B instead? As it turns out, that is precisely what he *can* do. With an expenditure of only P dollars of his own money, he can buy enough of firm B's stock to give him a prospective income stream having the same mean and variance as above—and therefore will pay no more than the original P dollars per share for firm A.

Thus, if he adds to P dollars of his own funds the amount

$$\frac{PD}{V - D} = \frac{VD}{N(V - D)} \tag{3-11}$$

---

[6] Since the need to specify per-share variance recurs throughout our discussion, the appendix to this chapter provides a full derivation of equation (3–8).

dollars of borrowed capital—borrowed from his stockbroker, for example—he can purchase a total of

$$\left[P + \frac{PD}{V-D}\right]/P = 1 + \frac{D}{V-D} = \frac{1}{\left(1 - \dfrac{D}{V}\right)} \tag{3-12}$$

shares in firm B at P dollars apiece. Since each of those shares represents the right to receive the fraction $1/N$ of the total dividends Y of firm B every year, the prospective annual cash receipts of the owner of $1/[1 - (D/V)]$ shares come to

$$\frac{Y}{N\left(1 - \dfrac{D}{V}\right)}.$$

If he must pay interest to his broker at a rate r on the $VD/N(V-D)$ dollars he has borrowed, his *net* annual income is

$$y_B = \frac{Y}{N\left(1 - \dfrac{D}{V}\right)} - \frac{rVD}{N(V-D)} \tag{3-13}$$

$$y_B = \frac{Y - rD}{N\left(1 - \dfrac{D}{V}\right)}, \tag{3-14}$$

and this set of prospective receipts therefore has a mean and variance equal to

$$\bar{y}_B = \frac{\bar{Y} - rD}{N\left(1 - \dfrac{D}{V}\right)} \tag{3-15}$$

$$\sigma^2(y_B) = \frac{\sigma^2(Y)}{N^2\left(1 - \dfrac{D}{V}\right)^2}, \tag{3-16}$$

which are exactly the same as those associated with one share of stock in firm A. Accordingly, there is no reason for our man to pay more than P dollars a share for the latter, and the stock of a levered firm should not sell at a premium.

AN ILLUSTRATION

A numerical example might prove helpful. Consider two firms, each of whose future total annual earnings are described by the simple probability distribution:

Possible Annual Earnings, Y	Probability of Y
$1.1 million	$\frac{1}{3}$
1.0 million	$\frac{1}{3}$ $\overline{Y}$ = $1.0 million
.9 million	$\frac{1}{3}$

Both firms have, say, 100,000 shares outstanding initially and neither has any long-term debt in its capital structure. Assume further that the per-share market price of both stocks is $100. Since the mean of prospective earnings per share in both cases is $10—$1.0 million spread over 100,000 shares—the implicit market discount rate, α, is 10 percent:

$$\alpha = \frac{\overline{Y}/N}{P} = \frac{\$10}{\$100} = .10.$$

And, finally, at $100 per share, the aggregate market value of both firms is $10 million. These numbers are quite arbitrary and are chosen merely because they are convenient to work with. Any set of alternative assumptions would do as well.

Let firm A then issue $5 million in long-term debt at an interest rate of 5 percent per annum. It uses the $5 million to repurchase and retire 50,000 shares of its stock at $100 per share. Since it must pay 5 percent of $5 million, or $250,000 per year, to its creditors, the probability distribution of total annual earnings available to the remaining shareholders becomes

$Y - rD$	$Pr(Y - rD)$
$850,000	$\frac{1}{3}$
750,000	$\frac{1}{3}$
650,000	$\frac{1}{3}$

With 50,000 shares still outstanding, the per-share prospects are therefore

$(Y - rD)/N_A$	$Pr[(Y - rD)/N_A]$
$17	$\frac{1}{3}$
15	$\frac{1}{3}$
13	$\frac{1}{3}$

Query: Will a share of stock with this probability distribution of future earnings—and dividends, assuming full earnings payout—sell for more than the original $100?

Answer: No, since an individual investor can duplicate that set of prospects by spending only $100 of his own money, borrowing $100 from his broker, and buying *two* shares of stock in still-unlevered firm

B. Thus, those two shares will provide him with an income stream with the following features:

$2Y/N_B$	$Pr(2Y/N_B)$
$22	$\frac{1}{3}$
20	$\frac{1}{3}$
18	$\frac{1}{3}$

Because, with 100,000 shares outstanding and no interest payments to meet, all of firm B's earnings are available to its stockholders. Our investor, however, must pay $5 per year to his broker for the $100 he has borrowed—assuming he also is charged 5 percent for his personal borrowing. His net income prospects therefore are

$(2Y/N_B) - r(100)$	$Pr[(2Y/N_B) - r(100)]$
$22 - $5 = $17	$\frac{1}{3}$
20 - 5 = 15	$\frac{1}{3}$
18 - 5 = 13	$\frac{1}{3}$

Which distribution is exactly the same as that provided by one share of stock in firm A. Accordingly, the latter cannot command a price greater than $100 even with its use of debt because, for an expenditure of only that amount, an investor can obtain the same income stream. He will not be willing to pay firm A to do for him that which he can as easily do for himself with personal leverage.

Two implications of this argument are worth noting. First, the investor who borrows to buy shares in firm B ends up having the same degree of *personal* leverage as firm A has *corporate* leverage. The debt-equity ratio for both is 1:1. Second, he owns the same proportion of the common stock of the corporation involved in both cases —1/50,000 of firm A or 2/100,000 of firm B. These results, of course, follow directly from the process of obtaining two equivalent income streams.

AN ALTERNATIVE VIEWPOINT

Another way of looking at that process would be to consider the opportunities available to an individual who has $200 to invest. He could, on the one hand, buy two shares of stock in firm B and thereby lay claim to the annual income stream:

Possible Income, $2Y/N_B$	*Probability*
$22	$\frac{1}{3}$
20	$\frac{1}{3}$
18	$\frac{1}{3}$

As an alternative, he could *lend* $100 of his funds to firm A—for example, by purchasing $100 worth of the $5.0 million in bonds the company has just issued. This would guarantee him an annual income of $5. How much, then, will he be willing to pay for one share of stock in firm A? Clearly, only the $100 he has left, since that share would add either $17, $15, or $13 to his annual income and give him the same combined set of outcomes as if he spent all his money on two shares in firm B. We therefore can prove our point in any one of several ways. The implication is that, whatever an investor's attitude toward borrowing and lending, he can always duplicate the results of the firm's capital structure decisions by taking an offsetting action of his own.

ADDITIONAL LEVERAGE

At this juncture, however, the reader may be disposed to protest: How about a *third* alternative? What about having an investor borrow to buy shares in levered firm A? Won't he be even better off, and therefore be willing to pay a premium for levered shares after all? Again, the answer must be no. He can always run fast enough to catch up simply by borrowing a little more from his broker and buying into firm B.

Consider the following: our man takes $100 of his own funds, borrows $100 from his broker, and buys two shares in firm A. Deducting his $5 interest costs, his new annual income prospects become:

y_A	$Pr(y_A)$
$34 − $5 = $29	$\frac{1}{3}$
30 − 5 = 25	$\frac{1}{3}$
26 − 5 = 21	$\frac{1}{3}$

If he borrowed $300 from his broker, added to it $100 of his own money, and bought *four* shares in firm B he would obtain:

y_B	$Pr(y_B)$
$44 − $15 = $29	$\frac{1}{3}$
40 − 15 = 25	$\frac{1}{3}$
36 − 15 = 21	$\frac{1}{3}$

and would again be in an equivalent position. Once more, our investor's proportionate ownership interest will be the same either way— 2/50,000 or 4/100,000—and so will be the degree of corporate *plus* personal leverage on the one hand (firm A) and personal leverage on the other (firm B). Regardless of his investment objectives and risk-taking preferences, he need not pay more for the shares of a levered firm to achieve them.

QUALIFICATIONS

There are, however, at least three things that could be wrong with this argument. One is that the individual investor may not in fact be able to borrow at the same rate of interest as a corporation can. The latter might have to pay only 8 or 9 percent for its funds, while an individual would be charged 10 percent or more. If this is the case, there *will* be an advantage to having the corporation do the borrowing and shares in levered firms will sell at a premium. That premium is likely to be rather small, though, as the reader can show by going through the example above using a different, higher r for personal borrowing.

A second objection might be that an individual may be held to a lesser degree of leverage relative to his own capital than is true of a corporation. His broker—or his bank—may not be willing to advance him the necessary sums to play the game described in the preceding sections. This does not seem a legitimate argument, however, for several reasons. For one thing, the examples given represent fairly extreme situations. Not many firms in our economy have a debt-equity ratio as great as 1:1. Most industrial enterprises are considerably below that figure, making the process of personal borrowing rather easier than the numbers above suggest. A more important point is that in most instances it really would not be necessary for an individual actually to borrow to buy unlevered shares. Most investors do not keep all their funds tied up in common stock. They have some portion of their portfolios deposited in savings accounts, in government bonds, or similar secure interest-bearing obligations. They are, in effect, normally lending part of their funds to the business community to begin with. Instead of having to borrow to purchase shares in firm B they can simply take some money out of their savings accounts or sell off some of the bonds they hold. Since this sort of "unlending" has exactly the same effect as borrowing, the impact on our investor's income prospects is equivalent, and he can choose whatever personal debt-equity ratio he desires for a given stock purchase. Indeed, this suggests that the interest rate discrepancy referred to above is not a problem either. If the investor has been lending to his bank at 4 percent, withdrawing some of his funds is just like borrowing at 4 percent on the margin.

Finally, an individual might not regard personal borrowing in the same light as corporate borrowing. If the firm borrows and goes bankrupt, all the investor stands to lose is the amount of the purchase price of his stock. If *he* borrows, he loses not only that sum but must repay his broker or his bank the principal amount of his personal loan. Once again, this appears a weak objection. The prospect of bankruptcy is not a very realistic concern for most large, well-established corporations—certainly not for those 2,500 or so which are traded on the nation's major securities exchanges and which give rise not only to the bulk of the country's economic output but the vast majority of its stock market activity. While for a small, new enterprise this issue is definitely relevant,[7] it is not a burning concern for us here.

SUMMARY

We conclude, then, that in a tax-free world, a corporation's debt-equity ratio should have no effect on its stock price—and, by inference, no effect on its cost of capital.[8] The composition of its long-term financial structure will be quite irrelevant to its shareholders. They can do everything for themselves through personal borrowing that the firm can do via corporate leverage. As we shall see, however, the introduction of taxes into the discussion changes this conclusion substantially.

APPENDIX: DERIVATION OF THE PER-SHARE VARIANCE EXPRESSION FOR A LEVERED FIRM

If the aggregate annual earnings of a levered firm are denoted by Y, its annual interest obligations by rD, and if it has $N\left(1 - \left[\dfrac{D}{V}\right]\right)$ common shares outstanding, its per-share annual earnings can be expressed as

$$y_A = \frac{Y - rD}{N\left(1 - \dfrac{D}{V}\right)}. \tag{A-1}$$

Since r, D, N, and V are constants, this expression may be rewritten in the form

---

[7] And at least partially explains the attempt made in Chapter 1 to confine our discussion to larger firms. See pp. 5–6 and Roland Robinson, *Financing the Dynamic Small Firm* (Belmont, Calif.: Wadsworth Publishing Company, Inc., 1966).

[8] Explicit consideration of the latter item will be deferred to the final model, which includes the role of taxes.

$$y_A = a_1 Y - a_2, \qquad (A\text{--}2)$$

where

$$a_1 = \frac{1}{N\left(1 - \dfrac{D}{V}\right)} \qquad (A\text{--}3)$$

$$a_2 = \frac{rD}{N\left(1 - \dfrac{D}{V}\right)} \qquad (A\text{--}4)$$

in order to simplify the subsequent algebra.

The task, then, is to derive an expression for the variance of y_A. By definition:

$$\sigma^2(y_A) = \Sigma(y_A - \bar{y}_A)^2 \, \Pr(y_A). \qquad (A\text{--}5)$$

That is, the variance of y_A is equal to the sum over all y_A observations of the squared deviations from the mean, each weighted by its probability of occurrence, $\Pr(y_A)$. If we can substitute in terms of Y for the several quantities on the right-hand side of this equation, we can express $\sigma^2(y_A)$ as a function of Y.

Conveniently, the probability that per-share earnings, y_A, will take on any particular value y_A^* is exactly equal to the probability that aggregate earnings, Y, will take on the corresponding value Y^*. Thus, if the probability distribution of Y is

Y	$Pr(Y)$
\$1.1 million	$\frac{1}{3}$
1.0 million	$\frac{1}{3}$
.9 million	$\frac{1}{3}$

and, following the example used in Chapter 3:

$$a_1 = \frac{1}{N\left(1 - \dfrac{D}{V}\right)} = \frac{1}{(100,000)\left(1 - \dfrac{\$\,5M}{\$10M}\right)} = \frac{1}{50,000}$$

$$a_2 = \frac{rD}{N\left(1 - \dfrac{D}{V}\right)} = \frac{(.05)\,(\$5M)}{50,000} = \$5$$

we have, as the probability distribution for y_A:

$y_A = a_1 Y - a_2$	$Pr(y_A)$
\$17	$\frac{1}{3}$
15	$\frac{1}{3}$
13	$\frac{1}{3}$

Hence:

$$\begin{aligned}
\Pr(y_A = 17) &= \tfrac{1}{3} = \Pr(Y = \$1.1M) \\
\Pr(y_A = 15) &= \tfrac{1}{3} = \Pr(Y = \$1.0M) \\
\Pr(y_A = 13) &= \tfrac{1}{3} = \Pr(Y = \$\ .9M)
\end{aligned}$$

or, in general:

$$\Pr(y_A = y^*_A) \equiv \Pr(Y = Y^*). \qquad \text{(A–6)}$$

Similarly, the mean of y_A is equal simply to a_1 times the mean of Y, less a_2:

$$\bar{y}_A = \$15 = \frac{\$1.0M}{50,000} - \$5 = a_1\bar{Y} - a_2.$$

Therefore we have everything we need to transform equation (A–5). Substituting in that equation:

$$\sigma^2(y_A) = \Sigma[a_1Y - a_2) - (a_1\bar{Y} - a_2)]^2\Pr(Y) \qquad \text{(A–7)}$$

$$\sigma^2(y_A) = \Sigma(a_1Y - a_1\bar{Y})^2\Pr(Y) \qquad \text{(A–8)}$$

$$\sigma^2(y_A) = a_1^2\Sigma(Y - \bar{Y})^2\Pr(Y). \qquad \text{(A–9)}$$

The term $\Sigma(Y - \bar{Y})^2Pr(\bar{Y})$ is, of course, nothing more than the variance of Y. Accordingly, we have

$$\sigma^2(y_A) = a_1^2\sigma^2(Y) \qquad \text{(A–10)}$$

$$\sigma^2(y_A) = \frac{\sigma^2(Y)}{N^2\left(1 - \dfrac{D}{V}\right)^2}, \qquad \text{(A–11)}$$

which is equation (3–8).

4

DEBT AND EQUITY:
TAX EFFECTS

When we take into account in our analysis the fact that corporations are taxed on their net income—but that any interest charges they incur are tax deductible—we find that the firm's debt-equity mix does have an impact on its stock price. In particular, the judicious use of debt financing should increase share prices since it is no longer possible for individual investors to duplicate the results of corporate borrowing through their own actions.

CORPORATE LEVERAGE

Let us return to our situation of two firms of the same size in the same line of business and start again with both having no long-term debt on their balance sheets. If we denote the corporate income tax rate by the symbol t_c, the aggregate market value of the common stock of both firms may be expressed as

$$V_t = \frac{\overline{Y}(1 - t_c)}{\alpha_t}. \tag{4-1}$$

α_t refers to the after-tax discount rate used by the market to evaluate a level annual income stream of the sort generated by firms in this risk class. On a per-share basis:

$$P_t = \frac{V_t}{N} = \frac{\overline{Y}(1 - t_c)}{\alpha_t N}, \tag{4-2}$$

where N denotes the number of shares outstanding for each firm. The subscript t will be carried throughout these expressions merely to distinguish the analysis from the no-tax model described in Chapter 3.

If firm A now decides, as before, to borrow an amount D at an interest rate r in order to retire the fraction D/V_t of its stock, the annual income available to each of its remaining shares becomes

$$y_A = \frac{(Y - rD)(1 - t_c)}{N\left(1 - \dfrac{D}{V_t}\right)}. \tag{4-3}$$

Thus, rD per year must be paid to creditors, leaving a total of $(Y - rD)$ for stockholders. The interest payments are tax-deductible, however, so that a net after-tax annual income of $(Y - rD)(1 - t_c)$ is provided.

The actual value for total before-tax earnings, Y, in any given year is a number produced by the relevant probability distribution of earnings for that year. Its possible outcomes therefore can be described for our purposes by a mean, $\overline{Y}$, and a variance, $\sigma^2(Y)$. Translating those parameters into their per-share counterparts, we have

$$\bar{y}_A = \frac{(\overline{Y} - rD)(1 - t_c)}{N\left(1 - \dfrac{D}{V_t}\right)} \tag{4-4}$$

$$\sigma^2(y_A) = \frac{(1 - t_c)^2 \left[\sigma^2(Y)\right]}{N^2 \left(1 - \dfrac{D}{V_t}\right)^2}, \tag{4-5}$$

since r, D, V_t, and N are again constants. The parameters $\bar{y}_A$ and $\sigma^2(y_A)$ also describe the stream of future *dividends* to be realized by the shareholders if, for the moment, we continue our assumption of full earnings payout.

PERSONAL LEVERAGE

The question, then, is whether an individual investor can lay claim to an income stream with the same features by borrowing to buy shares in unlevered firm B. If he were once more to use P_t of his own funds and borrow $P_t D/(V_t - D)$ from his broker at an interest rate r, he could purchase

$$[P_t + \left(\frac{P_t D}{V_t - D}\right)]/P_t = \frac{1}{1 - \dfrac{D}{V_t}} \tag{4-6}$$

shares of stock in corporation B. This action would provide him with a net annual income of size

$$y_B = \left(\frac{1}{1 - \dfrac{D}{V_t}}\right)\left(\frac{Y}{N}\right)(1 - t_c) - \frac{rP_t D}{V_t - D}. \tag{4-7}$$

Since $P_t = V_t/N$, that expression reduces to

$$\bar{y}_B = \frac{(Y - rD)(1 - t_c) - rDt_c}{N\left(1 - \dfrac{D}{V_t}\right)} \tag{4-8}$$

and its mean and variance are

$$\bar{y}_B = \frac{(\bar{Y} - rD)(1 - t_c) - rDt_c}{N\left(1 - \dfrac{D}{V_t}\right)} \tag{4-9}$$

$$\sigma^2(y_B) = \frac{(1 - t_c)^2[\sigma^2(Y)]}{N^2\left(1 - \dfrac{D}{V_t}\right)^2}. \tag{4-10}$$

This income stream, however, is inferior to that associated with a share of stock in firm A. The variances of the two are equal (equations 4–5 and 4–10), but the mean of y_B is lower (equations 4–4 and 4–9). An investor would therefore incur the same "risk" either way— according to our use of variance as an index of risk—but would have to settle for a lower expected annual return if he borrowed to buy into firm B. In consequence, a levered corporation's shares should command a higher market price than P_t.

AN EXAMPLE

A numerical example may again serve to clarify the argument. Consider two firms, each of whose aggregate annual before-tax earnings are described by the probability distribution:

Possible Earnings, Y	Pr(Y)
$1.1 million	$\frac{1}{3}$
1.0 million	$\frac{1}{3}$
.9 million	$\frac{1}{3}$

If both are unlevered, and we assume the corporate tax rate to be 50 percent, the after-tax earnings distribution for each is simply one-half of the above magnitudes with the same probabilities attached. The after-tax mean therefore is $500,000. With both companies having 100,000 common shares outstanding, their per-share market prices will be identical. Let us say this price is $50 per share, which implies an after-tax market discount rate for both of

$$\alpha_t = \frac{\bar{Y}(1 - t_c)/N}{P_t} = \frac{\$5}{\$50} = .10, \tag{4-11}$$

or 10 percent. The total market value of both firms is $5 million—
100,000 shares at $50 per share.

Now, firm A borrows $2.5 million at 5 percent interest, retiring
50,000 of its shares. Its new probability distribution of after-tax annual earnings available to common shareholders becomes:

$(Y - rD)(1 - t_c)$	$Pr[(Y - rD)(1 - t_c)]$
$\$(1.1 - .125)(.50) = \$487,500$	$\frac{1}{3}$
$(1.0 - .125)(.50) = 437,500$	$\frac{1}{3}$
$(\ .9 - .125)(.50) = 387,500$	$\frac{1}{3}$

since $.125 million in interest per year must be paid to creditors in
return for the $2.5 million borrowed. On a per-share basis, therefore,
the distribution for every future year is

$y_A = (Y - rD)(1 - t_c)/50,000$	$Pr(y_A)$
$\$9.75$	$\frac{1}{3}$
8.75	$\frac{1}{3}$
7.75	$\frac{1}{3}$

An investor who instead took $50 of his own money, borrowed $50
from his broker, and bought two shares in unlevered firm B would
obtain the distribution

$2[Y(1 - t_c)/100,000]$	$Pr(2[Y(1 - t_c)/100,000])$
$\$11$	$\frac{1}{3}$
10	$\frac{1}{3}$
9	$\frac{1}{3}$

This distribution, after deducting the $2.50 annual interest payments
he must meet, becomes

y_B	$Pr(y_B)$
$\$8.50$	$\frac{1}{3}$
7.50	$\frac{1}{3}$
6.50	$\frac{1}{3}$

He thereby is $1.25 worse off under every possible outcome, even
though the *dispersion* of those outcomes is the same as in the instance
of y_A. He will, accordingly, be willing to pay more than $50 for a share
of stock in the levered firm.

SOME COMMENTS

The factor which produces this result, of course, is simply that
peculiarity of our federal income tax law which stipulates that interest
payments by corporations are a deductible business expense. If such

were not the case, our analysis would show that there would still be no advantage to be gained through the use of debt financing. Alternatively, if it were possible to design a tax system under which an individual investor could receive a credit against his own tax for performing the same level of borrowing as the corporation does, we would also return to an equivalent position again. In either event, the point should be stressed that it is the corporate income tax *alone* which makes corporate leverage beneficial in terms of common stock prices. The fact that debt carries a low interest rate is not, in itself, a relevant consideration, if individual investors can also borrow at comparably low rates. The importance of this point explains the decision here to begin with a no-tax model in developing the analysis.

Any differences between the interest charges on personal and corporate borrowing would, as noted in Chapter 3, reinforce the current argument and make corporate leverage look even better. Similarly, the "limited-liability" feature of corporations—i.e., investors are not held personally responsible for corporate debts in bankruptcy but *are* liable for their own borrowings—adds further support in the context of small enterprises. The impact of these latter two factors, however, is likely to be quite small in relation to the tax effect, which is our main concern.

Finally, *personal* income taxes turn out to be of no consequence. Each of the formulas derived here would simply be multiplied by the factor $(1 - t_p)$ if personal taxes were recognized explicitly,[1] and none of the comparisons would be changed.

LIMITS ON LEVERAGE

While we conclude that the substitution of borrowed funds for shareholders' capital should produce a favorable effect on the price of a firm's (remaining) shares, there is obviously a limit to how far this argument can be carried. At its extreme, it would suggest that the corporation should keep issuing debt and retiring more stock until there is but one share left. That share would then sell at a very high price. Apart from the legal constraints the firm would eventually confront in doing this—there *are* limits on how much repurchasing of stock is permissible—there is a more practical constraint which would take hold much earlier: creditors would simply refuse to lend the firm any more money past a certain point. The company would reach a

---

[1] Or, by $(1 - t_p)^2$ in the case of the variance equations. t_p denotes the relevant personal tax rate.

position of not being able to promise to meet its annual interest obligations with any degree of confidence, and its supply of additional debt would be shut off.[2]

We see evidence of this type of reaction every day. The banks, insurance companies, pension funds, and other organizations which provide the bulk of the debt finance for corporations have developed a set of informal—and sometimes not so informal—guidelines with respect to how much debt firms in different lines of business can stand in relation to their equity capital. Not only do these guidelines place limits on the amount of borrowing that can be done, but, because they are recognized by the investment community as a whole, the people who buy common stocks also begin to worry when a firm approaches its generally accepted debt limit. They become less attracted to its shares because they perceive themselves being subjected to substantially increased risks of bankruptcy or reorganization in the event interest payments cannot be met, and the favorable effect on the firm's stock price no longer materializes.

We might depict the problem as in Figure 4–1. This chart represents, for a single firm, the relationship between its stock price and the level of its borrowing. When it approaches the point denoted its "debt

FIGURE 4–1. *Stock price effects of leverage.*

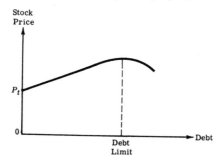

limit," the price increases forecast by our model above will become less attainable.[3] Eventually, the price is likely to fall as a result of the market's displeasure with the additional borrowing. In reality, of course, there is no one figure that could be agreed upon by all

___

[2] In effect, potential lenders would begin to feel that they were becoming exposed to some of the variability inherent in the corporation's earnings as the firm's aggregate annual interest obligations began to comprise a significant fraction of its expected annual income.

[3] And the interest rate charged by lenders will begin to increase as a reflection of their growing concern with the ability of the firm to meet its interest obligations.

concerned as *the* debt limit for a particular firm. Instead of the vertical line shown, some range of possible debt levels would make more sense as an indication of the maximum permissible amount of borrowing. However, the notion of a debt limit is no less real because it is often hard to identify exactly. Industry norms *have* been established, and a corporation ignores them at its peril—even if it can find a willing lender.

In terms of our model, the process could be viewed as follows: the firm keeps borrowing and retiring stock until its annual interest obligations rise to a level where they begin to require so much of the firm's total earnings that the latter are no longer sufficient to attract new creditors. In the illustration above, for instance, there was a one-in-three chance that total earnings in a given year might be only $900,000 before taxes. If the firm borrowed so much that its interest charges reached $900,000 per annum, it is unlikely that any additional lenders would be forthcoming. Our example, of course, is a contrived one. It would be more realistic to specify a probability distribution of earnings for the firm which included some values in the range of, say, $100,000 or even some negative possible outcomes. Business losses, after all, are not unknown. In such a case, it would be quite possible for the firm to foresee difficulties in meeting its interest obligations at a fairly low level of debt. We do not necessarily require that there be *no* chance of the firm's ever having a year in which its earnings are below its interest charges. It can always get through a temporarily depressed period by using short-term loans to cover long-term obligations, by using some of its excess cash to pay interest, or by cutting back production and selling off its inventory. We do insist—or, rather, its creditors would insist—that its interest obligations stay at a level where the probability of an earnings decline to a lower level is sufficiently small that only a temporary problem would be encountered. It is this sort of reasoning that underlies the notion of a debt limit.[4]

DEBT MATURITY

It has been assumed, at least implicitly, in the foregoing discussion that the firm, when it borrows, does so forever. No maturity date was

[4] And this explains why firms in lines of business that produce relatively stable earnings are able to borrow more than those whose earnings can vary widely from year to year in response to changes in external economic conditions. A public utility company, for example, will enjoy a higher debt limit than a manufacturer of automobiles or television sets.

identified for the loans involved. We treated the amount D as a perpetual loan, and the interest charges rD as if they were to be present indefinitely. While corporate debt does, of course, mature at some point and must be repaid, this consideration is no problem in terms of our model. We would simply say that, if borrowing has a beneficial effect on the firm's stock price as long as the amounts involved are within the relevant debt limit, a new loan should be obtained immediately to replace any old one which matures. Business practice supports that attitude. Corporations which use long-term debt as a matter of policy are continually refinancing their obligations as they come due. Public utility companies are an especially good example of this phenomenon.

STOCK RETIREMENT VERSUS NEW INVESTMENTS

It should also be pointed out that our examination of the debt-equity choice in the context of a firm using borrowed funds to retire common stock is only a strategy of expositional convenience. It permits us to ignore the asset investments on the left-hand side of the various balance sheets by holding them constant for two comparable firms. The conclusions reached do not depend on this approach. We could as well begin our analysis with two firms of the same size with similar income prospects, both having 50,000 shares outstanding. They both could then decide to undertake a set of identical new investments costing $2.5 million, but firm A would be assumed to finance those projects with debt while firm B would issue an additional 50,000 shares of stock at $50 per share. This would put us back to the position described above, and the relationships outlined would still hold. If the reader is more comfortable viewing the process in this manner, he should do so. It *is* necessary, whatever our approach, to be able to compare the two firms in an equivalent investment position ultimately if we are to isolate the effects of alternative financing decisions. But it makes no difference whether we achieve this result by talking about stock repurchases or by considering the financing of similar additional investments.

THE VALUATION EQUATION

If a firm's stock price may be expected to rise in response to its use of debt financing, the next question is: By how much? The answer can be found by deriving the basic market valuation equation for a levered firm subject to taxes.

Consider such a firm. With a total (expected) annual before-tax income equal to $\overline{Y}$ and debt outstanding in the amount D, the expected after-tax annual income available to its shareholders will be

$$\overline{Y}_S = (\overline{Y} - rD)(1 - t_c), \tag{4-12}$$

where again t_c denotes the corporate tax rate. The annual income anticipated by the firm's creditors is

$$\overline{Y}_D = rD, \tag{4-13}$$

and therefore the total after-tax income generated for both classes of security holders by the firm every year will be

$$\overline{Y}_T = \overline{Y}_S + \overline{Y}_D \tag{4-14}$$

$$\overline{Y}_T = (\overline{Y} - rD)(1 - t_c) + rD, \tag{4-15}$$

all in terms of the *mean* values of the relevant probability distributions. Since the only probabilistic item in the formulation is Y, the "mean" of the stream rD is simply rD itself.

What will be the total market value of such a firm? We saw above that the investing public used the discount rate α_t to appraise the worth of a level annual income stream generated by an unlevered firm in this risk class. That is, given the nature of the probability distribution of Y—and the existence of a corporate income tax—we found that the market value of such a corporation could be expressed as[5]

$$V_U = \frac{\overline{Y}(1 - t_c)}{\alpha_t}. \tag{4-16}$$

It should also be true, then, that if a portion of the income stream produced by our *levered* firm has the same characteristics—same $\overline{Y}$ and $\sigma^2(Y)$—that portion will be appraised similarly. This is indeed the case. If we rearrange equation (4-15) and break it down further, it becomes

$$\overline{Y}_T = \overline{Y}(1 - t_c) - rD(1 - t_c) + rD \tag{4-17}$$

$$\overline{Y}_T = \overline{Y}(1 - t_c) + rDt_c. \tag{4-18}$$

The piece $\overline{Y}(1 - t_c)$ has exactly the features we are looking for. The other portion, rDt_c, represents a guaranteed series of payments. Its

[5] From equation (4-1).

market value should therefore reflect the discount rate which the community applies to such payments—the rate r. If creditors lend the firm an amount D in return for an annual payment of size rD, they are implicitly telling us that a guaranteed income stream of that magnitude has a present value equal to D, as

$$D = \sum_{t=1}^{\infty} \frac{rD}{(1+r)^t} = rD \sum_{t=1}^{\infty} \frac{1}{(1+r)^t} = \frac{rD}{r} = D. \qquad (4\text{-}19)$$

An annual payment rDt_c will, by the same reasoning, be worth

$$\frac{rDt_c}{r} = Dt_c, \qquad (4\text{-}20)$$

and, in consequence, the aggregate market value of an income stream consisting of the two components $\bar{Y}(1 - t_c)$ and rDt_c will be just

$$V_L = \frac{\bar{Y}(1 - t_c)}{\alpha_t} + \frac{rDt_c}{r} \qquad (4\text{-}21)$$

$$V_L = \frac{\bar{Y}(1 - t_c)}{\alpha_t} + Dt_c \qquad (4\text{-}22)$$

$$V_L = V_U + Dt_c. \qquad (4\text{-}23)$$

The market value of a levered firm, V_L, when a corporation income tax is imposed is equal to the market value of an unlevered firm in the same risk class, V_U, *plus* the term Dt_c. The latter represents, in effect, the discounted present value of the tax savings resulting from the deductibility of the firm's interest charges. Because equation (4-22) is also the key to a determination of the cost of debt and equity funds to the company, it deserves particular attention.

IMPLICATIONS OF THE VALUATION FORMULA

We can see that this expression suggests a set of conclusions which are consistent with the statements made thus far about the effects of a firm's financing decisions. If there were no corporate tax—i.e., $t_c = 0$—equation (4-22) would reduce to

$$V_L = \frac{\bar{Y}}{\alpha_t} = V_U \qquad (4\text{-}24)$$

and leave us with the result indicated in Chapter 3—namely, that leverage cannot raise stock prices. The total market values of levered and unlevered firms would be identical, and every dollar's worth of debt issued to retire common stock would be matched by a corresponding reduction in the total market value of the remaining shares, thus leaving per-share prices unchanged.

The formula also implies that, when taxes are present, the more debt the firm incurs to retire stock the higher will be its total market value and therefore the higher its stock price per share. This is precisely the conclusion reached above. Each additional dollar of debt does *not* induce an offsetting decline in total market value under these conditions and the remaining shareholders gain. Similarly, the higher t_c is, the more powerful this effect since the tax advantages of a given amount of debt become that much greater.

We may then use equation (4–22) or (4–23) to predict the actual impact on per-share prices. To return to our example of firms A and B, we found that the total market value of each when they were unlevered was $5 million—100,000 shares at $50 per share. After firm A obtains its $2.5 million in debt, its new total market value should be

$$V_L = \$5.0M + (\$2.5M)(.50) = \$6.25 \text{ million}, \qquad (4\text{–}25)$$

and since it uses the funds to retire 50,000 of its shares, the price of those remaining becomes

$$\frac{\$6.25M - \$2.5M}{50,000} = \$75.00 \text{ per share}. \qquad (4\text{–}26)$$

Of the total $6.25 million in market value, debt accounts for $2.5 million, and the rest necessarily accrues to the common stockholders. In this manner, the effect of any level of debt we choose can be forecast, so long as the amount involved is within the debt limit referred to earlier. Figure 4–1 above is simply a graph of the per-share price implications of equation (4–22) for different values of D.

THE COST OF DEBT AND EQUITY

We are now in a position to determine the cost of the two forms of capital. As was pointed out in Chapter 1, "cost" in this connection refers to the rate of return which investments financed by either debt or equity must earn in order to justify acquiring the capital to undertake them. If they do not provide that return—i.e., if their present values are negative when calculated using the cost of capital we shall compute as the discount rate—the firm's shareholders will have been made worse off. As always, our criterion for shareholder welfare is stock price.

In this light, we may express the relevant criterion as follows:

$$\frac{\Delta V_T}{\Delta I} \geqq 1. \qquad (4\text{-}27)$$

The increase in the total market value of the firm, ΔV_T, which results from undertaking a new investment, must be at least as great as the dollar amount of the funds raised for that investment, ΔI. To illustrate: a firm with 50,000 shares of stock outstanding issues 5,000 additional shares at the prevailing market price of $50 per share and uses the $250,000 thus obtained to buy a new machine. Unless the prospective earnings increase generated by that machine induces the investing public to place a $250,000 higher value on the firm as a whole, the original—and also the new—stockholders will suffer a loss. The price of their shares can remain at $50 only if the firm becomes worth $2,750,000 in all, since 55,000 shares are now in existence. Similarly, if $250,000 in debt were raised for the new machine, the firm would also have to be valued at $2,750,000 after the investment. With that $250,000 outstanding, the other $2,500,000 in market value would just maintain a $50 stock price on 50,000 shares. The condition $(\Delta V_T / \Delta I) \geqq 1$ therefore neatly summarizes our requirements. It specifies the criterion which any new investment must meet in order to be acceptable to the firm's shareholders. If $(\Delta V_T / \Delta I) = 1$, they just break even.

Applying this criterion to our market valuation formula (4–22), we have

$$\frac{\Delta V_T}{\Delta I} = \frac{\Delta V_L}{\Delta I} = \left(\frac{\Delta \overline{Y}}{\Delta I}\right)\left(\frac{1 - t_c}{\alpha_t}\right) + \left(\frac{\Delta D}{\Delta I}\right)(t_c) = 1. \qquad (4\text{-}28)$$

The factors over which the firm has control are its anticipated earnings, $\overline{Y}$, its debt, D, and the investment expenditure, ΔI. The remaining items are constant insofar as the investment decision is concerned. From this expression, we can determine the minimum acceptable rate of return on a project as a function of the method chosen to finance it. The quantity we are interested in is

$$\frac{\Delta \overline{Y}}{\Delta I}(1 - t_c),$$

which we shall denote by the symbol R and which has the dimensions of a percentage figure.[6] This represents the increment to the firm's

---

[6] For example, an investment costing $1,000 which promised to add $200 per year before taxes and $100 per year after taxes to a company's earnings would imply an R equal to 10 percent. $\Delta \overline{Y}$ would be $200; ΔI would be $1,000; and t_c is 50 percent.

expected after-tax annual earnings which will result from the new investment—in short, the rate of return on that investment. The value for R which permits the condition $(\Delta V_T/\Delta I) = 1$ to be satisfied is the solution to the cost of capital question.

Thus, if an investment were to be financed entirely with new equity capital—a new common stock issue—the ratio $(\Delta D/\Delta I)$ in equation (4-28) would be equal to zero. No additional debt would be involved in the transaction, and our criterion would become

$$\frac{R}{\alpha_t} + (t_c)(0) = 1. \tag{4-29}$$

The R which meets this condition is simply

$$R = \alpha_t, \tag{4-30}$$

and we conclude that the required after-tax rate of return on an investment financed with equity—that is to say, the *cost of equity capital*—is equal to the after-tax discount rate applied by the investing public to the stock of an unlevered firm in the relevant risk class.

If the investment were financed with debt instead, we would have $(\Delta D/\Delta I) = 1$ in equation (4-28) and would find that

$$\frac{R}{\alpha_t} + t_c = 1 \tag{4-31}$$

$$R = \alpha_t(1 - t_c). \tag{4-32}$$

The required after-tax return on debt-supported projects—otherwise known as the cost of debt capital—is just $(1 - t_c)$ times the indicated cost of equity. We shall designate these two figures R_D and R_E in order to distinguish them in our discussion.

A more common circumstance, of course, would be one in which the firm had a *group* of proposed investments to consider and would like to raise a portion of the total funds needed through additional debt and the remainder via equity.[7] If we let L represent the debt portion, we have $(\Delta D/\Delta I) = L$ and our equation becomes

$$\frac{R}{\alpha_t} + t_c L = 1 \tag{4-33}$$

$$R = \alpha_t(1 - t_c L), \tag{4-34}$$

[7] This is also a more meaningful way to look at the cost of capital for a firm which intends to keep a mix of debt and equity on its balance sheet as it expands over time. The notion of a "debt-financed" or an "equity-financed" investment is less appropriate than the notion that *all* the firm's investments are jointly supported by both types of funds. This point is covered in some detail in Chapter 6.

which is the average cost of a package of debt and equity—call it R_A. It may also be written as

$$R_A = R_E(1 - L) + R_D L, \qquad (4\text{–}35)$$

which can be reduced to equation (4–34).

COMMENTARY

All these arguments follow from the market valuation formula (4–22). For that reason, it is necessary to keep in mind both the context and the limitations of the analysis which led to that equation. We talked throughout of comparisons between two firms in the same line of business—the same "risk class." Accordingly, when we speak here of the required return on a new investment, we mean an investment in the same general line of business that the firm currently is in. Otherwise, our framework breaks down and the capital costs indicated are not really the ones we want.[8] Any projects which the firm undertakes that are in the nature of expanding or maintaining its present activities, however, fit nicely into this mold. Since that list should certainly account for the bulk of aggregate corporate capital expenditures each year, we do have a useful criterion.

A second point to stress is that we always confront the problem of the firm's "debt limit." All our formulations are valid only if the levels of borrowing involved fall within the range considered appropriate for our company by the market. Because additional leverage should be beneficial until the upper end of that range is reached, the firm clearly should attempt to stay as close to it as possible. This may not be as difficult as may be suggested by our rather vague discussion above of the determination of the debt limit. We as financial managers can get some pretty reliable feedback from the institutions which lend us money. Our banker will simply refuse further loan requests when he thinks we have enough leverage—or the investment banker who has been marketing our bonds will inform us that we really ought to issue stock the next time we need large amounts of capital. While we may disagree with their appraisals, they are the people whose decisions the investment community respects. Their attitudes—not ours—are therefore the relevant ones in connection with stock price effects. Put crudely, then, the recommendation here for the financial manager is simply: Borrow as much as you can. If you don't have any good

---

[8] We shall return to this question in Chapter 7.

investments to spend the money on, retire some of your common stock; the market will tell you when to stop.[9] If the firm acts in this manner, it not only should maximize its share price—as much as it can through capital structure decisions—but will also minimize its "cost of capital." Both results are produced by the same leverage process. The firm's average cost of capital, R_A, as expressed by equation (4–34) will be lower the higher we can make its proportion of debt financing, L.

SECURITIES ISSUES

A final footnote to the preceding analysis relates to the mechanical problems in issuing new securities. While the underwriting and legal expenses connected with an offering of corporate bonds are quite small in comparison with the dollar amount of capital raised and can legitimately be ignored here, the same is not true of a new stock issue. Typically, the investment banker through whom we sell such an issue will find it necessary not only to charge us for his operating costs but will have to price the shares to be sold somewhat below the prevailing market price of our existing stock in order to ensure a rapid and successful sale. For a large corporation, this may well mean that the net proceeds realized by the company will be anywhere from 3 to 10 percent below the prevailing market price. The effect is to raise the true cost of new equity capital, R_E, by the same amount. If we let b denote this percentage gap between the theoretical and actual proceeds, we have as a revised figure for R_E:

$$R_E = \frac{\alpha_t}{1 - b},\tag{4-36}$$

and for the average cost of a package of new debt and equity:

$$R_A = R_E(1 - L) + R_D L\tag{4-37}$$

$$R_A = \frac{\alpha_t(1 - L)}{(1 - b)} + \alpha_t(1 - t_c)L,\tag{4-38}$$

from equation (4–35).

---

[9] Actually, the optimum strategy for a firm would be to stay "borrowed up" to just a little short of the point where it perceives its debt limit to be. This would leave a cushion of borrowing power to take care of emergencies or to permit the firm to act quickly on a good investment opportunity that may suddenly appear.

MEASURING THE COSTS

Even if the foregoing is accepted as an appropriate framework, however, the question as to whether the capital costs for a given firm can be measured from observable financial data must still be faced. Is it possible to come up with some numbers in an actual situation which will allow us to determine R_D and R_E? In order to accomplish this, it is first necessary to rearrange certain of the formulas above since none of them is quite yet in a form directly suitable for measurement purposes.

We may begin with our basic equation (4–22), which expresses the total market value of a levered firm. Given its current earnings expectations and the debt it has issued, its aggregate worth should be

$$V_L = \frac{\bar{Y}(1 - t_c)}{\alpha_t} + Dt_c. \qquad (4\text{–}22)$$

This total is, of course, also equal to the sum of the current market value of the firm's common stock, V_S, and the market value of its debt, D. We may therefore write

$$\frac{\bar{Y}(1 - t_c)}{\alpha_t} + Dt_c = V_S + D. \qquad (4\text{–}39)$$

Transposing the term Dt_c:

$$\frac{\bar{Y}(1 - t_c)}{\alpha_t} = V_S + D(1 - t_c). \qquad (4\text{–}40)$$

If we then multiply both sides of the equation by α_t and divide by V_S, we obtain

$$\frac{\bar{Y}(1 - t_c)}{V_S} = \alpha_t + \alpha_t(1 - t_c) \left(\frac{D}{V_S}\right). \qquad (4\text{–}41)$$

Finally, if the term $rD(1 - t_c)/V_S$ is subtracted from both sides—an operation which has no particular intuitive appeal but which is roughly equivalent to "completing the square" in algebraic factoring problems —the expression becomes:

$$\frac{\bar{Y}(1 - t_c)}{V_S} - \frac{rD(1 - t_c)}{V_S} = \alpha_t + \alpha_t(1 - t_c) \left(\frac{D}{V_S}\right) - \frac{rD(1 - t_c)}{V_S}. \qquad (4\text{–}42)$$

Combining terms:

$$\frac{(\bar{Y} - rD)(1 - t_c)}{V_S} = \alpha_t + (\alpha_t - r)(1 - t_c) \left(\frac{D}{V_S}\right). \qquad (4\text{–}43)$$

We thereby produce an expression into which current financial data can be fed and from which α_t can be calculated. The ratio

$$\frac{(\bar{Y} - rD)(1 - t_c)}{V_S}$$

is nothing more than the reciprocal of the firm's existing price-earnings ratio. Its expected before-tax annual earnings are $\bar{Y}$, its interest obligations amount to rD, and the corporate tax rate is t_c. Per-share expected earnings therefore are $(\bar{Y} - rD)(1 - t_c)/N$, where N denotes the number of shares it has outstanding. Its stock price is simply the total market value of its common shares, V_S, divided by N, and we have

$$\frac{(\bar{Y} - rD)(1 - t_c)/N}{V_S/N} = \frac{EPS}{P_t}, \qquad (4\text{--}44)$$

expected earnings per share over per-share stock price. If we denote that ratio by K, equation (4–43) becomes

$$K = \alpha_t + (\alpha_t - r)(1 - t_c)\left(\frac{D}{V_S}\right). \qquad (4\text{--}45)$$

Since we can determine every item in this structure of relationships from available market data except α_t, the latter can be solved for and used in the equations above. Thus, we can in fact compute our firm's cost of capital on the basis of what we are able to observe about the investing public's current reaction to its earnings prospects.

THE NUMBERS

The term D/V_S in equation (4–45) is simply the ratio of the market value of our outstanding debt to the total market value of our common stock. Both figures can be obtained from the financial section of our morning newspaper. If we have reason to suspect that today's stock price is somewhat out of line with what we think is its "normal" price because of a variety of temporary external factors that are influencing stock market conditions, we might use the average price over the last few months instead. The market value of our debt should fluctuate very little, however—and should be quite close to its "book" value as well.[10]

---

[10] In the event of any differences between the book value and the market value of the firm's debt, the latter is always the relevant figure since our whole analysis here is cast in terms of market attitudes. If the firm's debt issues are not traded publicly and, hence, no current market quotation is available, an estimate can be made simply by multiplying the book value of each of those issues by the ratio of their coupon rate of interest to the current market rate

The figure to be used for r is just the average rate of interest we are presently paying for our debt.[11] It can be derived in a situation where several different loans or debt issues are outstanding simply by dividing their aggregate current market value into the total annual interest payments required. The corporate tax rate t_c, of course, is given.

The only problem we may encounter is in arriving at a meaningful value for K. In addition to the matter of some temporary "noise" in the stock market—which we can probably handle by the sort of stock price averaging suggested above—there is the point that the earnings per share figure relevant for K is not necessarily *this* year's earnings. Rather, it is that level of earnings which the investment community believes will occur in the future. Investors have produced our current stock price by purchasing and selling shares according to their expectation of the success of our subsequent operations—which implies that we must determine what those expectations are and use *that* figure in calculating K. This is not such a difficult task, however. If our firm is large enough to have its shares traded actively, almost certainly several investment advisory services will have made an analysis of our prospects and distributed that information to their customers. We can therefore find out what "informed" opinion believes our future earnings will be and adopt the consensus of these estimates as our figure for $\overline{Y}$. The argument is that most investors are likely to be using the same number in deciding how much our shares are worth.[12] On that basis, we have everything we need to compute α_t.

A MEASUREMENT EXAMPLE

Our ubiquitous firm A can once more be used as an illustration. After it borrows the $2.5 million to retire a portion of its common stock, we find that

---

on issues of similar size and maturity. Thus, if we let D_B denote the book value of the debt, r_C its coupon rate, and r_M the going market rate on comparable issues by other firms, we have

$$D_M = D_B\left(\frac{r_C}{r_M}\right),$$

where D_M represents the estimated market value of the debt issue in question. If it *were* traded publicly, the market price should approximate this figure.

[11] On the assumption, of course, that the firm can secure additional loans in the future at approximately the same average rate.

[12] It should be noted that this estimate may well differ from the expectations of the firm's management. Since the investing public's opinion has given rise to the stock price we observe, however, *that* opinion about future earnings—not management's—is the pertinent one in the present context.

$$V_L = \$6.25 \text{ million} \qquad r = 5 \text{ percent}$$
$$V_S = \$3.75 \text{ million} \qquad \bar{y} = \$1.0 \text{ million}$$
$$D = \$2.5 \text{ million} \qquad t_c = 50 \text{ percent}$$

and, therefore, if

$$K = \alpha_t + (\alpha_t - r)(1 - t_c)\left(\frac{D}{V_S}\right), \qquad (4\text{–}45)$$

we have

$$\frac{(\$1.0M - \$.125M)(.50)}{\$3.75M} = \alpha_t + (\alpha_t - .05)(.50)\left(\frac{\$2.5M}{\$3.75M}\right)$$

$$\alpha_t = .10,$$

which, of course, is the value we chose for α_t to begin with. Accordingly, this is not a "proof"—merely an illustration.

DIVIDENDS AND EARNINGS

It should be emphasized again that our analysis has assumed throughout that the firm pays out all its earnings each year to its shareholders as dividends. K therefore is both the firm's dividend yield *and* the reciprocal of its price-earnings ratio. This framework can, with little difficulty, be extended to the more typical situation in which the company retains some of its earnings for reinvestment and thereby exhibits a growing stream of earnings and dividends over time. We shall discuss the nature of that adjustment in Chapter 7. As it turns out, all that is necessary is to adopt a revised estimate for K. The remainder of our measurement equation (4–45) remains intact—as do our expressions for R_E and R_D in terms of α_t—and the conclusions of the current chapter continue to be the correct ones. An example of the application of these techniques to a more realistic business case history will also be offered in Chapter 7.

SUMMARY

We have started with the basic proposition that the appropriate criterion for shareholders' welfare is the market price of their stock. We have considered the probable impact of alternative capital structure decisions on that price by examining the effect of the firm's debt-equity ratio on the expected value and the variance of the income stream associated with its shares. Were it not for the corporate income tax, we would conclude that debt-equity ratios would be of no concern and that the degree of leverage chosen by a firm would not alter the price of its stock. The fact that a corporate tax does exist, however, suggests that leverage *should* be beneficial to shareholders. They are unable to do for themselves via personal borrowing that which the firm can do for them by corporate borrowing. The tax-deductibility of the firm's interest charges produces this result. As long as a corporation stays within its generally accepted debt limit, its shareholders stand to gain the more it takes advantage of debt financing. In a rational securities market, no other conclusion seems acceptable.

Within this framework, we find it possible not only to specify the "theoretical" cost of debt and equity capital for a firm, but to provide a scheme for measuring both. It is worth emphasizing that, even if the numbers required for such measurements cannot always be obtained with great precision, it is not necessary that we insist on the kind of accuracy that would permit us to carry the computations to the point where we measure α_t to the nearest .01 percent. If we can merely arrive at a fairly narrow range of values, we have already achieved a major objective. For example, we may be sufficiently unsure of the market's opinion about our firm's future earnings—or sufficiently unclear as to whether this week's stock price is affected by a host of external factors unrelated to our capital structure situation—that alternative assumptions about these matters generate a set of values for α_t ranging from 9 to 11 percent. This is not at all a cause for unhappiness. We can still make a great many important investment decisions with considerable confidence. The large majority of our capital budgeting present-value computations will produce the same answer—i.e., accept or reject the proposal—whether we use 9, 10, or 11 percent as the relevant "cost of capital." As long as we are reasonably sure that the number is not 5 percent—or 20 percent—we can function effectively. The measurement technique developed above is not so sensitive to alternative values for V_S, r, $\overline{Y}$, and so on that it cannot at least provide a usefully narrow range of possible costs to work with. Since the prospective returns from most investment projects the firm will confront are themselves difficult to predict precisely, there is no point in getting too excited about a little imprecision in the cost of capital. Indeed, if our environment were as predictable as all that, we wouldn't have much to worry about either on the investment or the financing side of the balance sheet, and the present volume would be quite unnecessary.[13] We cannot pretend to "solve" the financial manager's problems. We can only attempt to provide the kind of improved information that will reduce certain of his dilemmas to a tolerable level.

A final comment—which may cause some dismay—concerns the cost of debt capital, expressed above as

$$R_D = \alpha_t(1 - t_c). \tag{4-32}$$

It should be noted that nowhere in this formula does the *interest rate* on debt appear. The contention is that the determinants of the required return on a debt-financed investment are but two: the "risk class" the investment (or the firm) is in and the corporate tax rate. The reasoning behind this assertion follows from the fact that individual investors are able to borrow at rates of interest similar to those on corporate borrowing, thereby effectively neutralizing the apparent advantage of low nominal interest charges. Only the corporate tax makes corporate leverage a good idea. The firm therefore should borrow in preference to issuing new stock *regardless* of the interest rate involved, just so long as it remains under its debt limit.[14] If this argument can be accepted—and understood—the reader should have no trouble with the subsequent analysis.

---

[13] The reader may already have his own opinions about the latter issue.

[14] An indication that this limit is being approached, of course, is likely to be a steadily higher interest rate charged by the firm's creditors because of their increasing concern with the ability of the firm to meet its interest obligations each year. They demand a higher price as payment for incurring a greater risk of default. In that respect, the benefits of leverage are not entirely unrelated to interest rate levels—but the connection is an indirect one.

5

RETAINED EARNINGS
AND SHARE PRICES

The impact of a corporation's retained earnings policy on the price of its shares can be examined in much the same manner as the effect of its debt-equity ratio: by determining whether it is possible for an individual investor, through appropriate actions with his own securities portfolio, to duplicate the results of the firm's decisions. If it *is* possible, the stock of firms in a given risk class—i.e., whose future income streams are equally uncertain—should all sell for the same price per dollar of expected earnings even though they establish different dividend payout ratios. As a corollary, the cost of capital for all such firms will be identical and will be determined entirely by the characteristics of the risk class to which they belong. We shall see that these conclusions in fact hold for a situation in which there are no personal income taxes. The existence of such taxes, however, implies that both share prices and capital costs *will* depend on the individual firm's dividend strategy.

APPROACH

In order once again to isolate the effect of the financial decision we are most immediately concerned with, certain other features of the corporate environment will be held constant. Comparisons will be made, as before, between two firms of the same size having similar earnings prospects. In addition, the stipulation will be that both are completely equity financed so that we need not repeat the analysis of Chapter 4. While the leverage and retentions discussions could be combined without affecting the conclusions drawn from either, the arguments made are likely to be clearer if the two topics are treated separately.

CORPORATE RETENTIONS: THE NO-TAX CASE

Consider first an economy in which neither personal nor corporate income taxes exist. If we have two unlevered firms in the same line of business, both of the same size and initially paying out all their earning as dividends, the aggregate market value of the common stock of each will be

$$V = \frac{\bar{Y}}{\alpha}, \qquad (5\text{--}1)$$

where $\bar{Y}$ denotes the expected value of each firm's future annual earnings and α the market capitalization rate applicable to companies with such prospects. If both have the same number of shares outstanding, N, their per-share prices can be expressed as

$$P = \frac{V}{N} = \frac{\bar{Y}/N}{\alpha}. \qquad (5\text{--}2)$$

Suppose, then, firm A decides to retain the fraction f of its coming year's earnings. It plans to reinvest the sum in new projects which promise annual returns in subsequent years having the same expected value and same variance per dollar of expenditure as its present activities. To make the case even stronger, let us assume that these returns will be perfectly correlated with the outcome of the firm's existing investments. Thus, if the firm has 100,000 shares of stock outstanding selling in the market at $100 per share, and its probability distribution of future annual earnings is initially

Possible Y	Possible Y/N	Probability
$1.1 million	$11	$\frac{1}{3}$
1.0 million	10	$\frac{1}{3}$
.9 million	9	$\frac{1}{3}$

we can infer that

$$\alpha = \frac{\bar{Y}/N}{P} = .10.$$

We therefore are talking about an investment costing perhaps $100,000 which promises an expected annual return of 10 percent as described by the outcomes:

Possible ΔY	Pr(ΔY)
$11,000	$\frac{1}{3}$
10,000	$\frac{1}{3}$
9,000	$\frac{1}{3}$

This investment is expected to raise the company's new probability distribution of earnings to

Possible Y_2	Possible Y_2/N	Probability
$1,111,000	$11.11	$\frac{1}{3}$
1,010,000	10.10	$\frac{1}{3}$
909,000	9.09	$\frac{1}{3}$

In every case, the new earnings total will be precisely the scale factor $(1 + \alpha f)$ times the original figure, where f is also equal to .10 and represents the ratio of the $100,000 cost of the additional investment to the firm's expected earnings of $1 million for the coming year.

The argument is cast in these terms simply as a means of keeping the firm being examined in the same risk class both before and after the investment. In this way, the retained earnings decision is the only issue, and comparisons with another firm, B, in a similar line of business will be appropriate. Such a framework should not be too unrealistic or restrictive since any outlay undertaken by a corporation which merely expands the scale of its existing operations rather than diversifies its activities would fit the indicated pattern.

As a result of firm A's expenditure on the new project—which it promptly and with great fanfare announces to the investment community—its shareholders can look forward to receiving a per-share dividend payment in year 1 having an expected value equal to

$$d_{A1} = \frac{\bar{Y}(1 - f)}{N} \tag{5-3}$$

and a variance of

$$\sigma^2(d_{A1}) = \frac{(1 - f)^2 \sigma^2(Y)}{N^2}. \tag{5-4}$$

With the addition of the new investment, which is expected to produce income at the annual rate α, total earnings in every subsequent year should be

$$Y_2 = Y + \alpha f Y = Y(1 + \alpha f), \tag{5-5}$$

and, if we further assume that the company intends to pay out all *these* earnings as dividends—i.e., the only retention involved is in the first year—the per-share mean and variance of its earnings and dividends from year 2 onward will appear as

$$d_{A2} = \frac{\bar{Y}_2}{N} = \frac{\bar{Y}(1 + \alpha f)}{N} \tag{5-6}$$

$$\sigma^2(d_{A2}) = \frac{(1 + \alpha f)^2 \sigma^2(Y)}{N^2} . \qquad (5-7)$$

This analysis can readily be extended to a situation where the firm decides to retain the fraction f of earnings *every* year. The argument is that, if it turns out that retentions in the current year should not affect *today's* stock price, a similar analysis repeated at the beginning of every subsequent year will lead to the same result for that year as well. The conclusions we arrive at for the single-period retentions case therefore are applicable in a more general framework.

The question is whether a stream of future dividends having the features

Year	Expected Value	Variance
1	d_{A1}	$\sigma^2(d_{A1})$
2	d_{A2}	$\sigma^2(d_{A2})$
3	d_{A2}	$\sigma^2(d_{A2})$
.	.	.
.	.	.
.	.	.

which is now perceived by investors to be associated with each share of stock in company A, should cause the current price of that share to depart from its original value P. To answer this question, we may inquire whether an individual investor might obtain the same prospective income stream by purchasing a share of stock in firm B at the price P now and then reinvesting for himself a portion of the dividends he expects to receive.

PERSONAL RETENTIONS

Specifically, let us suppose he purchases one such share with the thought of using the fraction f of his first year's dividends to acquire an additional (perhaps fractional) share in company B at the end of the year.[1] The expected value and variance of his net cash receipts for the coming year therefore are

$$d_{B1} = \frac{\bar{Y}}{N} - \frac{f\bar{Y}}{N} = \frac{\bar{Y}(1-f)}{N} \qquad (5-8)$$

$$\sigma^2(d_{B1}) = \frac{(1-f)^2 \sigma^2(Y)}{N^2}, \qquad (5-9)$$

[1] The problem of fractional share purchases should cause no concern. If our man literally held only one share of $100 stock in firm B, he would indeed be hard pressed to spend, say, $5 of his first year's dividend receipts to buy an additional $\frac{1}{20}$ share. However, an investor typically owns a sufficient

since firm B has a policy of paying out all its earnings as dividends and our man plans to set aside the amount $f\bar{Y}$ for additional stock purchases. Now, if firm B's prospects are for a level annual earnings stream, the market's expectation will be that its shares will still be selling at the price P a year from today. Accordingly, our investor can expect to be able to acquire the fraction

$$c = \frac{f\bar{Y}/N}{P} \tag{5-10}$$

of an additional share then by reinvesting $f\bar{Y}$ of his dividends. Since we established initially that

$$P = \frac{\bar{Y}/N}{\alpha}, \tag{5-2}$$

we have

$$c = \frac{f\bar{Y}/N}{\bar{Y}/\alpha N} = \alpha f. \tag{5-11}$$

He can plan to purchase αf of an additional share, ending up with $(1 + \alpha f)$ in all and producing for himself a dividend stream beginning in year 2 having the characteristics

$$\bar{d}_{B2} = \frac{\bar{Y}(1 + \alpha f)}{N} \tag{5-12}$$

$$\sigma^2(d_{B2}) = \frac{(1 + \alpha f)^2 \sigma^2(Y)}{N^2}. \tag{5-13}$$

This, of course, is exactly the same sort of cash flow pattern which company A promises. The expected value and the variance are identical not only for the coming year but for all future years. We therefore conclude that a share of stock in firm A cannot sell for more (or less) than P dollars currently. Dividend policy *per se* will not affect market prices in a tax-free world as long as earnings are reinvested in projects in the same risk class as the firm's existing operations. An individual can do as well for himself by "retaining" his own earnings as the company can do for him.[2]

---

number of shares that his dividends *will* permit him to acquire an integral number of new ones if he so desires. We shall concentrate here on a single share merely as an illustration.

[2] The transactions costs—i.e., brokers' fees—incurred by the individual investor in purchasing additional shares of firm B's stock are ignored in this and subsequent discussions. The assumption is that they are not large enough in practice to affect significantly the relevant comparisons.

CORPORATE RETENTIONS: TAX EFFECTS

A rather different conclusion emerges when taxes are introduced. Consider again two unlevered corporations in the same line of business, of the same size, and initially having a policy of paying out all their earnings as dividends. If we let t_c denote the corporate and t_p the personal income tax rate, the after-tax annual dividend in prospect for the owner of one share of stock in either firm will be

$$d = \frac{Y(1 - t_c)(1 - t_p)}{N}, \qquad (5\text{–}14)$$

with a mean and variance equal to

$$\bar{d} = \frac{\bar{Y}(1 - t_c)(1 - t_p)}{N} \qquad (5\text{–}15)$$

$$\sigma^2(d) = \frac{(1 - t_c)^2(1 - t_p)^2\sigma^2(Y)}{N^2}. \qquad (5\text{–}16)$$

Given a stock price of P_t dollars per share for both companies, we may define the after-*corporate*-tax market capitalization rate for firms in this risk class as

$$\alpha_t = \frac{\bar{Y}(1 - t_c)/N}{P_t}. \qquad (5\text{–}17)$$

This is just the counterpart of the after-tax capitalization rate discussed in Chapter 4—and, in fact, is defined in precisely the same manner.[3] If we observe P_t and have a reasonably good estimate of $\bar{Y}$, we can calculate α_t.

Assume, now, that firm A tells the investment community that it will retain the fraction f of its coming year's profits and use the funds to expand its present operations. The owner of one share of its stock thereupon expects under the new policy to receive in year 1 a dividend whose after-tax probability distribution is described by the parameters

$$\bar{d}_{A1} = \frac{\bar{Y}(1 - t_c)(1 - f)(1 - t_p)}{N} \qquad (5\text{–}18)$$

$$\sigma^2(d_{A1}) = \frac{(1 - t_c)^2(1 - f)^2(1 - t_p)^2\sigma^2(Y)}{N^2}. \qquad (5\text{–}19)$$

[3] See p. 32, equation (4–1).

The company's planned retention of the amount $f\bar{Y}(1 - t_c)$ of its after-tax earnings should, in the eyes of investors, raise the level of its aggregate after-tax profits in each subsequent year to

$$\bar{Y}(1 - t_c) + \alpha_t f \bar{Y}(1 - t_c) = \bar{Y}(1 - t_c)(1 + \alpha_t f), \qquad (5\text{–}20)$$

if, as in the no-tax situation, the firm invests in projects whose expected rates of return, α_t, are equal to those it is currently engaged in.

As an illustration, take again the case of a corporation which has 100,000 shares of stock outstanding at an observed market price of $50 per share and whose probability distribution of total annual before-tax profits is

Possible Y	Pr(Y)
$1.1 million	$\frac{1}{3}$
1.0 million	$\frac{1}{3}$
.9 million	$\frac{1}{3}$

If the corporate tax rate is 50 percent, we have

Possible $[Y(1 - t_c)]$	$Pr[Y(1 - t_c)]$
$550,000	$\frac{1}{3}$
500,000	$\frac{1}{3}$
450,000	$\frac{1}{3}$

from which we can compute an after-tax expected value of $500,000 and determine that

$$\alpha_t = \frac{\bar{Y}(1 - t_c)}{NP_t} = \frac{\$500,000}{\$5,000,000} = .10.$$

The kind of reinvestment of earnings we are concerned with, then, is one in which the firm might retain $100,000—20 percent of expected profits of $500,000—in year 1, and use the money for additional production facilities in such a way as to raise the probability distribution of its annual profits in subsequent years to

Possible Pre-Tax Profit, Y_2	Possible After-Tax Profit, $Y_2(1 - t_c)$	Probability
$1,122,000	$561,000	$\frac{1}{3}$
1,020,000	510,000	$\frac{1}{3}$
918,000	459,000	$\frac{1}{3}$

In effect, the $100,000 outlay offers the following set of annual outcomes, which are perfectly correlated with the firm's present earnings:

Possible ΔY	Possible $(\Delta Y)(1 - t_c)$	Probability
$22,000	$11,000	$\frac{1}{3}$
20,000	10,000	$\frac{1}{3}$
18,000	9,000	$\frac{1}{3}$

This investment therefore promises to increase every potential aggregate after-tax profit figure from year 2 onward to $(1 + \alpha_t f)$ times the year 1 value.

The result is an annual after-tax earnings stream—and dividend stream, assuming no subsequent retentions—displaying the features:

$$\text{Expected value} = \bar{Y}(1 - t_c)(1 + \alpha_t f) \tag{5-21}$$

$$\text{Variance} = (1 - t_c)^2(1 + \alpha_t f)^2 \sigma^2(Y). \tag{5-22}$$

Putting this on a per-share basis and deducting personal taxes at the rate t_p, we have

$$\bar{d}_{A2} = \frac{\bar{Y}(1 - t_c)(1 + \alpha_t f)(1 - t_p)}{N} \tag{5-23}$$

$$\sigma^2(d_{A2}) = \frac{(1 - t_c)^2(1 + \alpha_t f)^2(1 - t_p)^2\sigma^2(Y)}{N^2}. \tag{5-24}$$

And the parameters of the cash dividend stream which an individual who owns one share of stock in firm A can look forward to become

Year	Expected Value	Variance
1	$\bar{d}_{A1}$	$\sigma^2(d_{A1})$
2	$\bar{d}_{A2}$	$\sigma^2(d_{A2})$
3	$\bar{d}_{A2}$	$\sigma^2(d_{A2})$
.	.	.
.	.	.
.	.	.

as expressed by equations (5–18), (5–19), (5–23), and (5–24).

SHARE PRICE INCREASES

The presence of personal income taxes, however, makes it necessary that we examine one additional aspect of the investor's circumstances: the fact that the market price of firm A's stock should be greater than P_t by the end of the coming year. If the firm reinvests a portion of its earnings in order to generate a higher level of profits and dividends, it obviously will be worth more per share after that action. In particular, if its after-tax income is expected to grow in subsequent years to a level $(1 + \alpha_t f)$ times the present level, its per-share price at the end of year 1 will be expected by investors to be simply $P_t(1 + \alpha_t f)$.

The same phenomenon could have been examined in the no-tax model we began with, but in that environment an increase in stock prices had no tax consequences for the individual security holder. If he started out with one share of stock in firm A, he could expect to complete the first year having received a dividend payment equal to $\bar{Y}(1 - f)/N$ and owning a share worth $P(1 + \alpha f)$ dollars. If he instead started with a share in firm B, he would expect to be paid $\bar{Y}/N$ in dividends, would plan to use $f\bar{Y}/N$ of that amount to purchase the fraction αf of an additional share, and end up with $(1 + \alpha f)$ such securities worth P dollars each.[4] The alternative prospects therefore were equivalent. The shares of both companies were expected to produce the same net cash flows and to provide the same dollar value of stock holdings at year end, since there were no tax assessments to interfere.

On the other hand, a firm which retains a portion of its earnings in a world where personal income taxes exist *does* subject its shareholders to a tax liability in connection with increases in the price of their stock. Individuals must pay a tax on any "capital gains" they experience when they eventually resell their shares. It therefore becomes important that we recognize the extent of that liability in discussing the impact on shareholders of earnings reinvestment by the firm. If the price of each share of firm A's stock is expected to rise to $P_t(1 + \alpha_t f)$ dollars at the end of year 1, the anticipated capital gain is just $P_t\alpha_t f$, and the resulting capital gains tax obligation becomes $t_g P_t \alpha_t f$, where t_g denotes the relevant tax rate. Since our federal tax law specifies that capital gains are to be taxed at one-half the ordinary personal tax rate—with a maximum effective rate of 25 percent—t_g will always be less than t_p, whatever the tax bracket of the individual investor. Because the tax need not be paid until he actually disposes of his stock, we must of course also take into account the implications of the postponement. As a matter of convenience, we shall defer making this adjustment until we have completed the necessary analytical framework.[5]

Our view of the expectations of an individual who owns one share of stock in firm A at the present time can therefore be summarized as

---

[4] See pp. 54–57 above.
[5] See below, pp. 63–64.

follows: he anticipates a first-year cash dividend having an after-tax expected value and variance equal to

$$\bar{d}_{A1} = \frac{\bar{Y}(1 - t_c)(1 - f)(1 - t_p)}{N} \qquad (5\text{--}18)$$

$$\sigma^2(d_{A1}) = \frac{(1 - t_c)^2(1 - f)^2(f - t_p)^2\sigma^2(Y)}{N^2} \qquad (5\text{--}19)$$

and looks forward to end-of-year stock holdings worth

$$W_A = P_t(1 + \alpha_t f) - t_g P_t \alpha_t f \qquad (5\text{--}25)$$

$$W_A = P_t[1 + \alpha_t f(1 - t_g)] \qquad (5\text{--}26)$$

after deduction of the projected capital gains tax liability. The notation W_A is adopted because we are, in effect, talking about our investor's end-of-year *wealth* position.

PERSONAL RETENTIONS IN A TAX ENVIRONMENT

We can now compare this set of expectations with those of a man who owns a share of stock in firm B. If he plans to reinvest the fraction f of the dividends he receives in year 1, the after-tax mean and variance of his first-year net cash income will be

$$\bar{d}_{B1} = \frac{\bar{Y}(1 - t_c)(1 - t_p)(1 - f)}{N} \qquad (5\text{--}27)$$

$$\sigma^2(d_{B1}) = \frac{(1 - t_c)^2(1 - t_p)^2(1 - f)^2\sigma^2(Y)}{N^2}, \qquad (5\text{--}28)$$

which parameters are exactly the same as $\bar{d}_{A1}$ and $\sigma^2(d_{A1})$. In this respect at least, a share in either company will provide the same prospective inflow—just as in the no-tax case.

At the end of year 1, however, the owner of one of firm B's shares can expect to have available only the amount

$$\frac{f\bar{Y}(1 - t_c)(1 - t_p)}{N}$$

to purchase additional shares, since he must pay personal income taxes on his dividend receipts. This means that he can anticipate being able to acquire at a price P_t only the fraction

$$c_t = \frac{f\bar{Y}(1 - t_c)(1 - t_p)/N}{P_t} \qquad (5\text{-}29)$$

of an additional share. Substituting for P_t from our original equation (5–17), we have

$$c_t = \frac{f\bar{Y}(1 - t_c)(1 - t_p)/N}{\bar{Y}(1 - t_c)/N\alpha_t} \qquad (5\text{-}30)$$

$$c_t = \alpha_t f(1 - t_p), \qquad (5\text{-}31)$$

and our man's wealth at the end of the year should come to

$$W_B = P_t[1 + \alpha_t f(1 - t_p)]. \qquad (5\text{-}32)$$

He will own $[1 + \alpha_t f(1 - t_p)]$ shares at a price P_t per share. Capital gains taxes are not relevant in this instance simply because he does not expect to enjoy any such gains.[6] His greater wealth is to be a result of buying more shares rather than as a product of higher share prices.

The conclusion must be, then, that the owner of a share in firm B has in prospect an *inferior* set of outcomes compared with his firm A counterpart. Their first-year dividend expectations are identical, but we see that:

$$W_A > W_B. \qquad (5\text{-}33)$$

That is

$$P_t[1 + \alpha_t f(1 - t_g)] > P_t[1 + \alpha_t f(1 - t_p)] \qquad (5\text{-}34)$$

as long as $t_p > t_g$. That condition is satisfied because capital gains *are* taxed at a lower rate than dividend receipts. A share of stock in a firm which retains a portion of its earnings and reinvests them in projects that promise the same returns at the same degree of risk as its existing line of business should command a higher price currently than a share in a firm which pays out all its earnings. Dividend policy *will* have an impact on stock prices when taxes are present.

COMMENTARY

For two reasons, this conclusion is somewhat understated as it stands. To begin with, the analysis assumes that the applicable capital gains taxes must be paid by a shareholder in firm A at the end of year

[6] On the assumption, it should be emphasized again, that firm B plans to pay out all its earnings as dividends in each future year.

1. This is not necessarily the case, implying that our value for t_g should be reduced to adjust for any deferral. We might do that in a very crude way by estimating the length of time a "typical" investor would hold his shares before reselling them. If, for example, three years were the relevant period, the ability to defer the tax for an additional two years past year 1 would mean that an investor would effectively be able to continue investing his tax liability in a risk class of firms whose income streams are capitalized by the market at the discount rate α_t. The present value as of the end of year 1 of a tax payment due two years later would therefore be

$$PV(t_g) = \frac{t_g}{(1 + \alpha_t)^2},$$ (5-35)

and, if α_t were equal to the 10 percent figure we have been using in our examples, the implication is that

$$PV(t_g) \approx .8t_g.$$ (5-36)

A 25 percent capital gains rate would really be only about a 20 percent rate in present value terms.

The second point is a related one. If we decide that a share of stock in firm A ought to sell for more than P_t dollars now according to the comparisons made above, the total capital gains tax liability incurred by its shareholders will be less than the amount $t_g \alpha_t P_t f$ assumed. The net price increase anticipated within year 1 from holding a share in firm A will not be

$$P_t(1 + \alpha_t f) - P_t$$

but instead

$$P_t(1 + \alpha_t f) - P'_t,$$

where $P'_t > P_t$. This supplies an additional reason for preferring to buy shares in firm A. That factor need not be incorporated explicitly into our analysis at this stage, however, since when we discuss the "cost" of retained earnings below, the question will be asked: What rate of return must firm A insist on from its new investments in order to produce a current price of *exactly* P_t? The adjustment will therefore be made in connection with a lower expected end-of-year price.

CORPORATE INCOME TAXES

While both personal and corporate income taxes have been included in the preceding discussion, it may be observed that the corporate tax rate drops out of the final comparisons. Only the parameters t_g and t_p appear in equations (5–26) and (5–32), which define the differences in expected year-end wealth positions. This result is similar to that indicated in Chapter 4 to the effect that *personal* income taxes are irrelevant to the firm's debt-equity choice.[7] On the one hand, it is the corporate-tax-deductibility of interest charges that leads us to our conclusions; on the other, the difference between the capital gains and the ordinary personal tax rates. If it were not for the latter difference, in fact, we would conclude that a firm's dividend policy would not influence its stock price even in the presence of taxes, since we would have $t_p = t_g$ and $W_A = W_B$. These observations are worth keeping in mind. They imply that the only reason the financial manager of a corporation ends up being confronted with financial strategy problems is that our government participates in a very distinctive way in the fruits of the firm's activities. We could, without much difficulty, design an alternative tax system that would make both dividend policy and leverage matters of no significance to either a corporation or its shareholders.[8]

AN OPTIMUM DIVIDEND POLICY

It is, however, necessary to hedge this last statement insofar as dividend policy is concerned. Even if there were no personal income tax—or if the capital gains rate were not lower than t_p—a firm obviously would still have to decide how much of its earnings to retain. The question as to whether profitable investment opportunities are available will always be pertinent. A corporation should refrain from paying dividends only if retained earnings can be put to work in projects which offer sufficiently high returns that its shareholders thereby gain. This, of course, is the "cost of capital" problem. The minimum acceptable rate of return on retention-financed investments—the cost of retained earnings—is simply that profit rate which will raise the price of the firm's stock by enough that, after capital gains taxes are deducted, its shareholders are as well off as if they had received a dividend payment instead and paid the associated personal income tax. This has been precisely the focus of our analysis thus far. We have compared the after-tax dividends-plus-capital-gains anticipated by firm A's stockholders with the after-tax dividends expected by those of firm B—some of the latter of which were to be reinvested. An

---

[7] See p. 36.
[8] If the reader can swallow this, he should be well prepared to accept what follows.

optimum dividend policy, then, is one in which all earnings that cannot be employed within the firm at rates of return at or above the relevant cost of capital are paid out to shareholders. We saw that firm A could raise the price of its stock (net of capital gains taxes) in excess of its shareholders' foregone (after-tax) dividends by reinvesting in projects which would earn at the same rate α_t as its existing operations. Clearly, there is some rate below α_t that will produce a stock price increase at which the shareholders will just break even. This figure is the cost of capital we seek.

DIVIDEND REINVESTMENT

Before going on to that issue, one further observation is in order. In comparing the income prospects of stockholders in the two firms considered, the stipulation was that the owner of a share in company B plan to reinvest some of his dividends in more shares of that company at the close of the first year. If we take this assumption literally and all firm B's shareholders decided to follow that strategy, there would almost certainly be a sudden increase in demand that would push up the price of its stock and raise some questions about our comparisons. It should be emphasized that this approach to the analysis is adopted only for purposes of illustration. Any one of several alternative viewpoints would serve as well. We could, for example, pose the problem in terms of having a shareholder in firm B use a portion of his dividends to purchase stock in some other company, C, in the same risk class. He would thereby obtain an income stream having the same mean and variance per dollar of expenditure as in the case of firm B and again be in an equivalent position. There are some potential problems with this approach unless we assume that firm C's earnings outcomes are perfectly correlated with firm B's—i.e., all companies in the same industry experience their good and bad years together—but it is not an unreasonable alternative and could be pursued.[9]

Perhaps the most salient point, however, is that we do not really need to talk about our investor's using his first year's dividends from firm B for reinvestment at all. We could cast up the comparisons by looking merely at the anticipated end-of-year wealth positions of two individuals, one of whom expects both to receive a dividend from firm A and experience a capital gain, and the other

[9] The issue involved concerns the manner in which the stock of firm A, B, or C fits into an investor's *total* securities portfolio. We shall raise this issue again in Chapter 8.

to receive a larger dividend from firm B with no capital gain. Whether the latter investor actually plans to reinvest a portion of his dividends or not is in fact irrelevant. He will be required to pay personal income taxes on the full amount received in any case, and can expect to end up with total net receipts for the year of only $\bar{Y}(1 - t_c)(1 - t_p)/N$ whatever his subsequent decisions. The dollar value of any additional shares he purchases must be exactly equal to the after-tax dividend income he spends on them. The reinvestment assumption therefore has been employed simply as a device to keep our comparisons as clear-cut as possible by rendering equivalent certain segments of the income streams involved. It is in that respect a matter of expositional convenience rather than a prerequisite to our conclusions. The numerical example offered below will further document this contention.

THE COST OF RETAINED EARNINGS

If the shareholders of firm A gain *vis-à-vis* those of firm B when earnings are retained for projects in the same risk class promising an annual rate of return α_t, the question is: What rate will leave them *just* as well off? What expected return can firm A accept in order that the after-tax dividends and capital gains anticipated by its owners during the coming year will be such as to lead the investment community to continue to place the value P_t on its shares now?

The question is easily answered since all we need determine is the rate of return which, in terms of the notation above, will produce the result

$$W_A = W_B. \tag{5-37}$$

We have already established that the characteristics of the prospective first-year net dividend receipts for investors in the two companies are identical if the shareholders of firm B plan to reinvest the same fraction f of their dividends as firm A reinvests of its earnings. That is:

$$\bar{d}_{A1} = \bar{d}_{B1} \tag{5-38}$$

$$\sigma^2(d_{A1}) = \sigma^2(d_{B1}). \tag{5-39}$$

Accordingly, if both sets of individuals can expect to end the year with the same after-tax wealth position as well, the shares of the two firms should sell for the same price currently.

Now, an expected after-corporate-tax return of α_t on new investments promised to raise firm A's stock price at year end to

$$P_2 = P_t(1 + \alpha_t f). \tag{5-40}$$

If the return—always for projects in the same risk class—were not α_t but some figure R_R, the price should be instead

$$P'_2 = P_t(1 + R_R f) \tag{5-41}$$

and the wealth of each of firm A's shareholders after deducting the capital gains tax liability associated with a price increase from P_t to P'_2 would become

$$W_A = P_t(1 + R_R f) - t_g[P_t(1 + R_R f) - P_t] \tag{5-42}$$

$$W_A = P_t[1 + R_R f(1 - t_g)]. \tag{5-43}$$

The condition to be satisfied, then, is

$$W_A = P_t[1 + R_R f(1 - t_g)] = W_B = P_t[1 + \alpha_t f(1 - t_p)] \tag{5-44}$$

for the stock of both firms to sell for P_t now. Solving for R_R:

$$R_R = \frac{\alpha_t(1 - t_p)}{(1 - t_g)}. \tag{5-45}$$

An expected after-tax rate of return equal to the factor $(1 - t_p)/(1 - t_g)$ times the after-tax market capitalization rate for firms in this risk class therefore represents the cost of retained earnings to such firms. If that return is available, their shareholders should be indifferent between a cash dividend payment or the investment project being considered.[10]

NUMERICAL EXAMPLE

Take the case of company A, which has 100,000 shares outstanding at a $50 per share market price, and whose future annual earnings and dividends are characterized by the probability distribution:

---

[10] The fallacy in the statement, still seen in some finance texts, that retained earnings are "free" to the firm should be clear from the foregoing discussion. It is true that the firm itself need not "pay" someone for those funds—but if we agree that the firm should be run for the benefit of its owners, the cost to them of retained earnings is that figure we have just derived. They give up a dividend payment when the firm retains funds and, unless the firm makes an investment which generates an equivalent capital gain, they lose.

Possible Before-Tax Earnings, Y	Possible After-Tax Earnings, $Y(1 - t_c)$	Probability
$1.1 million	$550,000	$\frac{1}{3}$
1.0 million	500,000	$\frac{1}{3}$
.9 million	450,000	$\frac{1}{3}$

From the expected value of after-tax annual earnings of $500,000 we can calculate α_t to be 10 percent, i.e., $\bar{Y}(1 - t_c)/NP_t$. If the relevant personal tax rate for the firm's shareholders were 40 percent, and the capital gains rate 20 percent, our analysis above would indicate that the cost of retained earnings is

$$R_R = .10 \frac{(1 - .40)}{(1 - .20)} = .075.$$

A retention-financed new investment in the same line of business which promised an expected annual return of 7.5 percent after corporate taxes would be acceptable. If the investment cost $100,000, it would have to promise the set of annual outcomes:

Incremental Pre-Tax Earnings	Incremental After-Tax Earnings	Probability
$16,500	$8,250	$\frac{1}{3}$
15,000	7,500	$\frac{1}{3}$
13,500	6,750	$\frac{1}{3}$

This would imply that the firm's annual earnings—and dividends—beginning in year 2 would be distributed as:

Possible Total After-Tax Earnings	Possible Per-Share After-Tax Earnings	Probability
$558,250	$5.5825	$\frac{1}{3}$
507,500	5.0750	$\frac{1}{3}$
456,750	4.5675	$\frac{1}{3}$

If a per-share earnings distribution of $5.50–$5.00–$4.50 now sells for $50, this one will be expected to sell for $50.75—an expected annual income of $5.075 capitalized at 10 percent. Armed with that knowledge, the current owner of one share of the company's stock will anticipate a 75-cent capital gain during the coming year as a result of its retained earnings. Because the firm has told him it will retain $1 per share for a total of $100,000, the dividend income he foresees is:

Possible Dividend	Probability
$4.50	$\frac{1}{3}$
4.00	$\frac{1}{3}$
3.50	$\frac{1}{3}$

These dividends are taxable to him at 40 percent. His expected capital gain will be taxed at 20 percent. Accordingly, his combined after-tax income prospects for year 1 are:

Possible After-Tax Income	Probability
($4.50)(.60) + ($.75)(.80) = $3.30	$\frac{1}{3}$
($4.00)(.60) + ($.75)(.80) = $3.00	$\frac{1}{3}$
($3.50)(.60) + ($.75)(.80) = $2.70	$\frac{1}{3}$

Compare that set of prospects with the outcomes offered the owner of a share of stock in a similar firm B, which intends to pay out all its earnings as dividends:

Possible Dividend	Dividend Minus Personal Tax at 40 Percent	Probability
$5.50	$3.30	$\frac{1}{3}$
5.00	3.00	$\frac{1}{3}$
4.50	2.70	$\frac{1}{3}$

This probability distribution is identical to that available from firm A. We could stipulate that an investor use $1 of each of these receipts to purchase an additional $\frac{1}{50}$ of a share in company B at year end.[11] This would give him a net dividend income of $2.30–$2.00–$1.70 plus a dollar's worth of increased stock holdings. Either way, his end-of-year after-tax wealth matches that of an investor in firm A. The stock of both companies should therefore sell for $50 per share currently.

Consider, finally, a third alternative. Another firm, C, in the same line of business also decides to undertake investments costing $100,000 but announces that it will issue 2,000 additional shares to provide the necessary funds. In that event, the new investments must promise the annual outcomes:

Incremental Pre-Tax Earnings	Incremental After-Tax Earnings	Probability
$22,000	$11,000	$\frac{1}{3}$
20,000	10,000	$\frac{1}{3}$
18,000	9,000	$\frac{1}{3}$

[11] The extra $\frac{1}{50}$ share would, in effect, raise his dividend prospects beginning in year 2 to the $5.5825–$5.075–$4.5675 distribution promised by firm A due to its retentions.

This will mean, with 102,000 shares outstanding by the end of the coming year, that firm C's prospects will be:

Total After-Tax Earnings	Per-Share After-Tax Earnings	Probability
$561,000	$5.50	$\frac{1}{3}$
510,000	5.00	$\frac{1}{3}$
459,000	4.50	$\frac{1}{3}$

This *must* be the case if each share is to continue to sell for $50. The firm's current shareholders can expect to receive either $3.30, $3.00, or $2.70 in after-tax dividends during year 1 and can plan to spend $1 on an additional $\frac{1}{50}$ of a new share if this condition is met. They will in that way be as well off as their counterparts in the other two companies. It turns out, then, that investments financed by new common stock issues must promise a 10 percent expected return rather than only the 7.5 percent acceptable if earnings are retained.[12]

RELATIONSHIP TO THE DEBT-EQUITY MODEL

That comparison points up the connection between the analysis of this chapter and that performed in Chapter 4 for the firm's debt-equity decision. We began in both instances by examining the effect on shareholders' income prospects of departing from the situation of an unlevered firm which paid out all its earnings as dividends. On the one hand, we maintained the dividend assumption but introduced the influence of borrowing. On the other, we changed dividend policy while continuing to exclude leverage. In each instance, we arrived at a cost of capital for the particular source of finance involved which was expressable in terms of some factor times the cost of equity—i.e., some factor times the market capitalization rate for unlevered firms in the relevant risk class. The α_t of the current chapter is the same α_t which was bandied about in Chapter 4. Its definition, as we saw in equations (4–1) and (5–17), is identical. We therefore have succeeded in establishing an interrelated hierarchy of capital costs represented by the following expressions:

---

[12] These figures, of course, depend on the tax rates we have assumed as well as on the numbers chosen for the example.

$$R_E = \frac{\alpha_t}{1-b} \tag{4-36}$$

$$R_R = \alpha_t \frac{(1-t_p)}{(1-t_g)} \tag{5-45}$$

$$R_D = \alpha_t(1-t_c), \tag{4-32}$$

where b denotes the percentage gap between the existing price of a corporation's stock and the net proceeds realized because any new shares must be "underpriced" in order to sell.[13] If we can estimate α_t for our company from observable market data, we can determine the cost of whatever form of finance it may choose—and we can seek to minimize its overall cost of capital by prescribing an appropriate mix of funds. Some indication of the nature of this process was outlined in Chapter 4 for the debt-equity decision.[14] Our concern in Chapter 6 will be to combine that framework with the retained earnings model and, in Chapter 7, to apply the resulting analysis to a more realistic business situation than the examples discussed thus far represent.

TAX RATES AND THE COST OF RETAINED EARNINGS

The key issue in measuring the cost of retained earnings, of course, lies in specifying appropriate values for the two parameters t_p and t_g. To a shareholder in a very high marginal personal income tax bracket, retained earnings will appear an exceedingly inexpensive source of funds for the firm. If his tax rate is, say, 70 percent and the maximum effective capital gains rate is 25 percent, the cost of retained earnings will from his standpoint be just $(1 - .70)/(1 - .25)$, or 40 percent of the theoretical cost of a new common stock issue.[15] Moreover, if the firm can realize only 90 percent of the prevailing market price of its stock from such an issue due to underwriting expenses and underpricing, retained earnings become

$$\frac{R_R}{R_E} = \frac{\alpha_t(1-t_p)/(1-t_g)}{\alpha_t/(1-b)} = \frac{(1-.70)(1-.10)}{(1-.25)} = .36,$$

[13] See p. 46 above.
[14] Pp. 48–50 above.
[15] In this and subsequent comparisons, the ability of a taxpayer to defer the capital gains tax will be ignored.

merely 36 percent as expensive as new equity. This would compare with a cost of debt capital of

$$\frac{R_D}{R_E} = \frac{\alpha_t(1 - t_c)}{\alpha_t/(1 - b)} = (1 - .50)(1 - .10) = .45,$$

45 percent that of equity, assuming a 50 percent corporate tax rate.

In contrast, an investor in a 20 percent personal tax bracket will perceive the following cost comparison:

$$\frac{R_R}{R_E} = \frac{(1 - .20)(1 - .10)}{(1 - .10)} = .80$$

$$\frac{R_D}{R_E} = (1 - .50)(1 - .10) = .45,$$

since capital gains are taxed to him at only 10 percent—half his ordinary personal tax rate. He will prefer that the firm use debt finance to the extent it can stay within its debt limit before retaining any earnings for additional investments. Clearly, the firm needs some information on the income-and-tax circumstances of its owners if it is to make an intelligent decision about the composition of its capital structure.

That information could perhaps be obtained by asking for it directly from the shareholders—through a survey conducted either by management or by some outside organization. A firm whose stock is actively traded and whose stockholder group is constantly changing, however, will find this approach to be of limited value unless the survey is repeated at frequent intervals. It may be costly to undertake such a program and, in addition, the information obtained may not be terribly reliable if shareholders are reluctant to respond to the necessary questions about their personal finances. A more sensible procedure would be simply to use the empirical evidence we do have about a "typical" investor as derived from aggregate stock ownership and income tax data. The most recent such data suggest that the average common stockholder is in a 30 percent marginal tax bracket, and that the associated effective capital gains rate—recognizing the fact that those gains are taxed only when realized rather than as accrued—is roughly 10 percent. This implies a retained earnings cost equal to

$$\frac{R_R}{R_E} = \frac{(1 - .30)(1 - .10)}{(1 - .10)} = .70,$$

approximately 70 percent of the cost of new equity finance—assuming an underwriting and underpricing gap of 10 percent. If a business firm regards its current and prospective stockholders as being generally representative of the average for the entire investment community, this figure is a reasonable one to use for decision-making purposes. We shall adopt that hypothesis here.

SUMMARY

We find, then, that it *is* possible to arrive at a set of capital costs for the three major sources of corporate funds.[17] In doing so, the question throughout has been: Can individual investors arrange their own securities portfolios in such a way as to achieve for themselves the results which the firm achieves by making certain financial decisions? We see that taxes end up standing in their way and produce a situation wherein both leverage and dividend strategies will have an important effect on share prices.

[17] The matter of the cost of preferred stock will be examined in Chapter 8. It has been put aside up to now mainly on empirical grounds. Very little preferred stock financing has been employed by business firms in recent years, and such securities no longer constitute a significant source of new capital for most companies.

6

THE AVERAGE COST
OF CAPITAL

In order to integrate the analysis of the preceding chapters, it is necessary to develop an expression for the overall cost of a capital structure which consists of various proportions of debt, retained earnings, and common stock issues. The problems involved in applying that framework to the circumstances of the individual firm also deserve more attention than they have been accorded up to now.

WEIGHTED AVERAGE COST

The cost of capital confronted by an enterprise which depends on all three types of long-term funds to support its operations can be calculated simply by weighting the cost of each by its relative importance. If a firm is contemplating a group of investment projects and proposes to raise the money to undertake them by using retained earnings as a source of the fraction X_R of the total capital required, by borrowing the fraction X_D, and by issuing additional common stock for the remaining fraction X_E, the weighted average cost of the funds is just

$$R_A = (X_R)(R_R) + (X_D)(R_D) + (X_E)(R_E), \qquad (6\text{--}1)$$

where R_R, R_D, and R_E denote the individual costs derived earlier. By definition

$$X_R + X_D + X_E = 1. \qquad (6\text{--}2)$$

The total funds raised must equal the total required for the new investments.

Substituting the relevant expressions in equation (6–1), we have

$$R_A = (X_R)(\alpha_t)\frac{(1 - t_p)}{(1 - t_g)} + (X_D)(\alpha_t)(1 - t_c) + (X_E)\frac{(\alpha_t)}{1 - b} \quad (6\text{-}3)$$

or

$$R_A = \alpha_t\left[X_R\frac{(1 - t_p)}{(1 - t_g)} + X_D(1 - t_c) + \frac{X_E}{1 - b}\right] \quad (6\text{-}4)$$

for the resulting weighted average. A similar formula was developed in Chapter 4 in connection with the choice between debt and new equity, but retained earnings had not yet been considered explicitly in that discussion.[1]

LONG-RUN AVERAGE COST

Since the firm is concerned with acquiring a package of funds to spend on a package of investments, there is nothing to be gained by unwrapping either package and attempting to associate a particular type of finance with a particular investment project. The firm is judged by the investing public not on an item-by-item basis but as an entity. Its stock price reflects the market's attitude toward the conse-quences of all its financing and expenditure decisions combined—be-cause those decisions produce only *one* result which is of interest to investors: an income stream that the owner of each share of the company's stock can expect to receive. From the market's standpoint, there is no such thing as a debt-financed investment or an equity-fi-nanced investment. There are only debt-financed companies and equity-financed companies which make investments and generate in-come. The mix of funds they choose "costs" the entire firm some annual percentage figure as determined from our examination of stock price effects, and summarized in the weighted average cost just derived. Every one of a corporation's assets must earn profits at that annual rate if its shareholders are to benefit. It is therefore idle to categorize such assets in terms of various individual sources of finance. The firm owns them all and its capital structure supports them all equally.

This conclusion applies not only to a single year's investments but to the long run as well. The securities market is not in the least interested in the fact that last year the firm happened to borrow the money which it spent on new plant and equipment while this year it issued common stock to finance further outlays. Shareholders observe only that a series of investments have been made and a mix of funds

[1] See pp. 44–45.

has been employed. The stock price which ensues depends on how the two fit together in the aggregate, rather than on the timing involved. Had common stock been issued first instead, and the borrowing been done this year, the firm's circumstances—and the market's reaction after the fact—would be no different. Both the company's balance sheet and its shareholders' income prospects would be the same.

When we undertake to calculate a weighted average cost of capital, then, we are concerned with the proportions X_R, X_D, and X_E which pertain in the long run as a firm expands its activities. The actual sequence in which capital is raised in arriving at those proportions is merely a matter of tactics and timing to take advantage of year-to-year changes in market conditions. If a firm's long-run target debt ratio is equal to 25 percent of its total capitalization ($X_D = .25$), that figure is the one we should use in determining its cost of capital. Every investment expenditure in every year must satisfy the resulting rate of return criterion, even if it turns out that all the money spent in a given year comes nominally from borrowing. That year's investments cannot be considered to be "debt financed" and thereby be allowed to pass a low rate of return test, because in the following year the company will have to either retain some earnings or issue more common stock in order to restore the desired balance to its capital structure. In that sense, every investment is eventually supported by the firm's long-run financing strategy and must be so treated.[2]

This contention is perhaps most difficult to accept in connection with an asset which is offered as collateral for a particular loan. If a company borrows money from a bank to build a warehouse, for example, and the bank takes a mortgage on the warehouse to protect its position, shouldn't that expenditure be considered as debt financed? The answer here is still no. The mortgage is merely a device to induce the bank to lend the funds and to permit the company to attain its desired overall debt ratio. The income stream produced for its shareholders is no different than it would be if some other asset were pledged as collateral—or if no collateral were offered at all. The market reacts only to the effect of the resulting interest charges on the firm's per-share earnings prospects. Investors are not buying separate shares of stock in a warehousing operation. They are buying a claim

---

[2] Another way of stating the same proposition is to note that if the firm adheres to a particular target set of proportions X_D, X_R, and X_E in its capital structure over time, its long-run average and marginal costs of capital will be identical. Both would be represented by the same horizontal line on a chart of capital costs versus the quantity of funds raised by the firm.

to the net profits of the entire company and they see just one income stream being produced. If the warehouse is a poor investment, it affects them in the same way any other poor investment does. They care very little how the firm managed to acquire its debt financing; their concern is simply that some aggregate interest obligations must be met every year out of earnings.[3]

AN OPTIMUM CAPITAL STRUCTURE

Given an expression for a corporation's weighted average cost of capital, the question then becomes: How does the firm minimize that cost? Clearly, by relying on the least expensive single source of funds for as much of its total needs as practicable. According to our discussion in the last chapter and the various tax rates we took to be relevant, debt finance emerges as the first choice. The comparison was

$$R_E = \frac{\alpha_t}{1 - b} = \frac{\alpha_t}{1 - .10} \doteq 1.1\alpha_t \qquad (6-5)$$

$$R_R = \alpha_t \frac{(1 - t_p)}{(1 - t_g)} = \alpha_t \frac{(1 - .30)}{(1 - .10)} \doteq .8\alpha_t \qquad (6-6)$$

$$R_D = \alpha_t (1 - t_c) = \alpha_t (1 - .5) \doteq .5\alpha_t, \qquad (6-7)$$

all in terms of the market capitalization rate, α_t, that is associated with the risk class to which the firm belongs. A corporation should simply borrow up to its debt limit and keep borrowing in that same proportion as it expands over time. The "equity" component of its capital structure should be supplied insofar as possible through retained earnings. Only if the firm still has available investment projects that promise a higher rate of return than the cost of capital which it calculates after exhausting its retentions should it resort to issuing more common stock. This, incidentally, is a recommendation that accords quite well with empirical evidence about business behavior. Most firms do in fact make use of borrowed funds to the extent they feel the market will countenance, and they much prefer to retain earnings rather than

[3] If we admit more than an infinitesimal possibility that the firm may go bankrupt, however, we do need to be less cavalier about the significance of assets pledged as collateral to creditors. Such a pledge is likely to result in a somewhat different set of outcomes for shareholders if the company fails and in that sense may affect their income prospects. Because the difference should not be too great—and because bankruptcy is being treated here as a pretty remote possibility—we shall not undertake to explore this issue.

sell additional common shares. The latter source of capital is widely regarded as by far the most expensive of the three.

The long-run average cost of capital for a corporation which perceives its debt limit to be, say, 25 percent of its total capitalization and which finds it necessary to secure outside equity finance sufficiently infrequently that only 10 percent of its funds are raised in that manner over the years will therefore be

$$R_A = (.25)(.5\alpha_t) + (.65)(.8\alpha_t) + (.10)(1.1\alpha_t) \qquad (6\text{–}8)$$

$$R_A \doteq .75\alpha_t. \qquad (6\text{–}9)$$

This is the figure the firm should use in calculating the present values of the investment opportunities it contemplates, as long as those projects are all in the same general area of business activity. Thus, a chemical company would use this approach in appraising additional expenditures on chemical-producing plant and equipment.

CAPITAL RATIONING

The suggestion is that any investment which offers an after-tax rate of return greater that R_A—or, alternatively, which has a positive net present value when its prospective after-tax cash inflows and outflows are discounted at the rate R_A—is desirable.[4] It should have the effect of raising the price of the corporation's stock. In theory, if the firm does not have enough funds after paying its regular dividend to take advantage of all the investments which pass this test in a particular year, it should immediately cut its dividend, borrow additional capital, and if necessary issue more common stock. That strategy should continue until all projects which promise a positive present value have been undertaken, even if it means an erratic dividend payment—or perhaps no payment at all in certain periods—and a widely varying aggregate capital budget from year to year.

In practice, of course, such a decision rule is unlikely to be followed. Corporations regard it as good policy to maintain a stable or steadily growing series of annual dividend payments. Neither are they attracted by the idea of issuing small amounts of common stock at frequent intervals. Rather than adjust their funds sources in the short run to their capital budgets, they adjust the capital budget, putting off

---

[4] These two procedures for evaluating investments are not quite equivalent even though they are treated here as interchangeable. For a fuller discussion, see Robert W. Johnson, *Capital Budgeting* (Belmont, Calif.: Wadsworth Publishing Company, Inc.).

some apparently worthwhile projects until the funds become available. If they are consistently generating more good investments than they can undertake, they may slowly reduce their dividend payout as a percent of earnings—by not raising the dividend as rapidly as earnings grow, for example—and may well float an issue of new common stock more often.

While this strategy might imply in principle some inefficiencies in the use of funds, it is not really very much at odds with our normative discussion here. It *is* sensible to look at the firm's operations from a long-range viewpoint and not get too excited about making short-run decisions which will appear to the investment community as eccentric behavior. The financial manager may know in his heart that a particular investment is an excellent idea and that his shareholders will be better off if he spends the money for it right away instead of maintaining the firm's current dividend payment. But the investment community may be more skeptical (or less knowledgeable), and it may be necessary to continue to "buy" their goodwill by not cutting the dividend and thereby postponing the expenditure until more money becomes available through appropriate longer-run adjustments in funds sources. This is the rationale for adopting a long-run weighted average approach to the cost of capital analysis. We are always interested in doing as well as possible for our shareholders by seeking increases in the price of their stock, but we may at times have to forego making rapid changes in our capital structure that seem desirable in theory in return for preventing unwanted short-term fluctuations in that same price. Certainly, the recommendation here would be that a firm which finds itself constantly in a "capital rationing" situation—having more good investments than available funds—should act over time to reduce its dividend payout ratio and, if necessary, issue more common stock at strategic intervals. It should also stay "borrowed up" to its debt limit. In this way, it will do more for its shareholders than if it instead continued to ignore worthwhile investments. The proposal is not, however, that the indicated adjustments be made overnight—just that the firm attempt to respond gradually and systematically to take advantage of its recurring profit opportunities.

DIVIDENDS AND THE CAPITAL BUDGET

The same sort of reasoning can be used to rationalize the phenomenon of dividend payments by firms which occasionally do resort to additional common stock financing. Our hierarchy of capital costs would suggest that retained earnings are a "cheaper" source of funds than such stock issues and that it would be better to eliminate the dividend entirely before going outside for more equity capital. Nonetheless, some dividend payments may be necessary in order to convince investors that good things are happening with the firm and that it is sensible for them to count on its long-run prosperity. Clearly, we observe corporations in different lines of business adopting quite different dividend payout ratios in what seems a logical pattern. Firms like electronics companies that appear to have numerous attractive investment opportunities do in fact pay out a much lower percentage of their earnings than corporations in more mature industries. Indeed, some pay no dividends at all for many years on the reasonable assumption that they can put their funds to work so profitably within the firm that their shareholders stand to benefit considerably more from the capital gains generated than from direct cash payments. The issue for a firm which feels itself capital rationed, then, is one of balancing the need to pay at least a nominal dividend which is intended to keep investors hopeful about—and interested in—its stock against the longer-run desirability of retaining earnings to minimize capital costs. Fortunately, the dilemma is not a terribly serious one. We shall see below that the average cost of capital for a corporation is not likely to be raised significantly if it chooses to use a little more outside equity finance than it might consider optimal in order that some modest dividends can be paid in the short run.

EXCESS CAPITAL

For certain firms, of course, the reverse of the capital rationing problem may exist. They may have more funds available for reinvestment after paying their "normal" dividend than they have good projects to undertake.[5] The appropriate strategy in that case is to do either of two things: return the excess to the shareholders or keep the money on hand for use in subsequent periods. The choice should depend on the firm's expectations about its future opportunities. If it feels that the surplus is a temporary phenomenon and that it will confront a rationing situation again soon, it probably makes more sense to put the money aside for a year or so—by investing it in marketable securities, for example—than to declare a "special" divi-

---

[5] This, by the way, is an unhappy situation. If the firm's management group can't find profitable uses for a large portion of its available capital, it may well imply that they're not looking hard enough or being imaginative enough—or both.

dend and then ask for the funds back by issuing common stock later. We could perform a precise analysis by comparing the returns a shareholder might obtain by investing the money himself with the eventual cost to him of a new common stock issue. Because a number of assumptions about both his and the firm's investment opportunities would be necessary to such an analysis, however, it does not seem really worthwhile getting involved in. We might as well simply assert that the funds should be kept on hand for use when capital rationing reappears.[6] This is consistent with our long-range viewpoint.

If, on the other hand, the firm frequently finds itself experiencing a surplus of capital, the conclusion must be that it's time to raise the dividend.[7] Shareholders will be better served if they are given the money to invest elsewhere than they will be by having the company accumulate idle cash or other redundant assets. Again, the transition to a new, higher dividend is perhaps best accomplished gradually—if for no other reason than the possibility that the firm might have been too pessimistic about its future investment opportunities and might wish several years later that it had more retained earnings to spend.

It should also be emphasized in this connection that it is more desirable to raise the dividend than to reduce permanently long-term borrowings. As long as the company is within its perceived debt limit, we have decided that debt is a less expensive form of capital than retained earnings. A firm therefore should use excess cash to pay larger dividends rather than repay loans. In fact, if any earnings at all are retained within the year, the appropriate strategy is to *increase* long-term borrowing so as to maintain the target proportion of debt financing previously established—even though this may mean that the firm's dividend is being increased at the same time.[8]

Consider the following situation: a firm earns $1 million after

---

[6] It may be pointed out that there is more than one way to keep such funds "on hand." The firm could reduce some of its short-term loans outstanding during a year when it has excess cash and then simply reborrow when funds needs become pressing again. The savings in interest charges thereby obtained are equivalent to interest earnings on short-term marketable securities. The decision should be made according to whether the firm can earn more on its securities portfolio than it is paying to its creditors. While this also suggests that the firm could repay a portion of its *long-term* debt temporarily and then reborrow those funds, it is likely to be the case that the nature of its contractual agreements with such creditors preclude this sort of manipulation.

[7] Or to repurchase some shares of its stock. We shall consider the relative merits of the two alternatives in Chapter 8.

[8] If this sort of proposal that the firm "borrow to pay dividends" sounds bizarre, it really isn't—and it continually occurs in practice. Any time a firm pays dividends during a year when its total outstanding loans have increased, it has in part at least borrowed money to pay dividends.

corporate taxes and interest charges in a given year. Its normal dividend payments total $500,000 and it has $400,000 worth of profitable investments to undertake. If its debt limit seems to be in the neighborhood of 25 percent of its total capitalization—and prior to the current year it has stayed "borrowed up"—what strategy is called for now? Answer: the firm should finance $300,000 of the $400,000 in good investments with retained earnings; it should borrow the other $100,000; and it should pay a total of $700,000 in dividends.[9] By so doing, it will continue to keep the cost of the capital it does need at a minimum by taking full advantage of its borrowing capacity.

SENSITIVITY OF CAPITAL COSTS

One of the issues relevant to this search for the most desirable capital structure for a firm concerns the severity of the penalties incurred if the financial manager does not quite pick the "best" possible combination of funds. Clearly, the nature of the problem is such as to suggest that there will always be more than a little imprecision in the analysis. A corporation's debt limit is likely to be difficult to identify exactly—and that limit may shift over time as the firm matures, as the character of its earnings changes, and as the attitudes of its creditors evolve. Similarly, the firm may wish to pay some modest level of dividends each year despite being capital rationed, thereby requiring more in the way of new outside equity finance eventually than would otherwise be the case. The question is: What price in terms of an increased cost of capital do the firm and its shareholders pay by either intentionally or inadvertently departing from a theoretically optimum capital mix?

A feeling for the orders of magnitude involved can be obtained by using the schedule of capital costs derived above and testing the impact on R_A of some alternative financial strategies a "typical" firm might choose. Thus, we have

$$R_D = .50\alpha_t \qquad R_R = .78\alpha_t \qquad R_E = 1.11\alpha_t$$

from equations (6–5) through (6–7), carrying out the calculations implied there to one additional significant digit.[10] Let us suppose our

---

[9] Or, in terms of the arguments made above, it should steadily increase its dividend to this level over several years if it feels the shortage of worthwhile investments will persist.

[10] This degree of "accuracy" of course is quite spurious and is adopted here only because many of the changes in R_A produced by a mild reshuffling of the firm's finances do not show up except in the last digit—which conclusion is in itself a fairly succinct comment on their importance.

firm's "correct" long-run capital structure would consist of the proportions: debt, 30 percent; retained earnings, 60 percent; common stock issued, 10 percent. That is, if the firm retained all its earnings and added to them debt and new equity funds in the indicated relationship, it could invest the full amount raised in projects which promise after-tax rates of return equal to or greater than

$$R_A = \alpha_t [(.30)(.50) + (.60)(.78) + (.10)(1.11)] \quad (6-10)$$

$$R_A = .74\alpha_t. \quad (6-11)$$

The debt figure of 30 percent is assumed to be the effective limit imposed by creditors—the firm has tested the capital markets often enough to be convinced that this figure really is the relevant ceiling.

Under these conditions, what would be the consequences if the firm decided to pay at least a nominal dividend even while expanding? Suppose that dividend—which reduces earnings available for retention—would require that the firm issue common stock more frequently than before and thereby cause the proportion of outside equity finance to rise over time to 20 percent of total capitalization. This would suggest a new average cost of capital equal to

$$R_A = \alpha_t [(.30)(.50) + (.50)(.78) + (.20)(1.11)] \quad (6-12)$$

$$R_A = .77\alpha_t, \quad (6-13)$$

which, obviously, is not startlingly higher than the original figure and is well within the limits of accuracy with which we can estimate α_t to begin with.[11]

A similar conclusion emerges if we examine the effect of a lower actual debt ratio than the 30 percent permissible. If the firm misreads its creditors' attitudes—or is simply nervous about potential adverse reactions in the stock market to that much debt—and ends up carrying only a 20 percent ratio, the missing funds must be replaced again by additional outside equity capital since the level of retained earnings is fixed. The R_A will be

$$R_A = \alpha_t [(.20)(.50) + (.60)(.78) + (.20)(1.11)] \quad (6-14)$$

$$R_A = .80\alpha_t, \quad (6-15)$$

[11] See Chapter 7 with regard to this measurement problem.

returning to the initial no-dividend situation. If the firm underestimates its debt ceiling *and* chooses to pay dividends, we have

$$R_A = \alpha_t [(.20)(.50) + (.50)(.78) + (.30)(1.11)] \qquad (6\text{–}16)$$

$$R_A = .83\alpha_t, \qquad (6\text{–}17)$$

and we do begin to observe a meaningful increase as compared with the minimum figure of $.74\alpha_t$. The more marked the departures from the preferred proportions 30–60–10 become, the steadily more expensive the firm's capital structure. While the extent of these variations certainly depends on the numbers chosen for this particular example, the relationships indicated are probably not too unrepresentative of the position in which most large manufacturing firms would find themselves. Alternative assumptions can easily be substituted by the reader.

STOCK PRICE EFFECTS

It should also be pointed out in interpreting these results that what may seem a fairly small change in R_A has rather more significant implications for the firm's stock price—which is our ultimate concern. For instance, we saw in Chapter 4 in discussing the effects of leverage that a firm which was entirely equity financed and had expected annual earnings of $1 million before taxes with 100,000 shares of stock outstanding would sell for $50 per share, assuming the relevant α_t was 10 percent.[12] Thus

$$P_t = \frac{\overline{Y}(1 - t_c)/N}{\alpha_t} = \frac{\$5}{.10} = \$50. \qquad (6\text{–}18)$$

The total market value of such a firm is $5 million. Suppose, then, it borrows an additional $5 million at 5 percent interest and simply doubles all its investments. It remains in the same "risk class" at twice the income level by so doing and its new total market value can be determined from the valuation formula

$$V_L = \frac{\overline{Y}(1 - t_c)}{\alpha_t} + Dt_c, \qquad (4\text{–}22)$$

where, now, $\overline{Y}$ is equal to $2 million but α_t is still 10 percent. Substituting, we find that

---

[12] Pp. 34–35. We are also assuming full dividend payout once again.

$$V_L = \frac{(\$2M)(.50)}{.10} + (\$5M)(.50) = \$12.5 \text{ million.} \qquad (6\text{-}19)$$

Accordingly, the market price of each of the 100,000 shares outstanding will be

$$P'_t = \frac{V_S}{N} = \frac{V_L - D}{N} = \frac{\$12.5M - \$5.0M}{100,000} = \$75, \qquad (6\text{-}20)$$

a 50 percent increase. The average cost of capital for the firm, however, has fallen only from 10 percent[13] to

$$R_A = \alpha_t[X_D(1 - t_c) + X_E] \qquad (6\text{-}21)$$

$$R_A = .10[(.5)(.50) + (.5)] \qquad (6\text{-}22)$$

$$R_A = 7.5 \text{ percent.} \qquad (6\text{-}23)$$

Thus a decline of 25 percent in R_A produces a 50 percent rise in P_t. A similar relationship would hold for any level of debt we might examine. A firm's stock price is indeed relatively more sensitive to changes in its finance mix than is its average cost of capital—and our interest in attempting to reduce that average even by a small amount through appropriate adjustments in funds sources is not without merit.

WEIGHTING THE COSTS

As the example above suggests, the correct weights to attach to the various forms of capital in computing R_A are those which define the importance of each as of the time they are *raised*. X_D, X_R, and X_E are book value proportions from the firm's balance sheet, not market values. The company described went to the capital markets twice. The first time was for $5 million in common stock,[14] the second for $5 million of debt. It is therefore *employing* a 50–50 debt-equity mix. The fact that the *result* of this choice is an increase in the market price of the firm's stock to $75 per share is obviously a happy circumstance, but it does not mean that the company raised $7.5 million in equity rather than only $5 million. It means that management was very clever in its capital structure decisions and has generated the type of outcome toward which our discussion has been directed.

---

[13] Ignoring for the moment the "underpricing" problem associated with common stock issues.

[14] Assuming the issue price was actually $50 originally.

This distinction between book and market values has perhaps been somewhat blurred up to now for one very simple reason. In determining capital costs, the question was asked: What rate of return will leave the firm's shareholders just as well off after the investment as before? What return will produce an increase in the total market value of the company which is exactly equal to the additional funds raised? In effect, our criterion was stated in terms of matching the market values of investments to their book values. We did not need to be very precise in identifying which we were talking about most of the time since both were the same as a condition of the relevant discussions. When we now recognize that the financial manager's basic objective is nothing more than to make the two diverge by inducing stock price increases, a different attitude is called for. The average cost of a package of funds, like the cost of any set of resources, depends on the importance of each form of capital in its role as an *input* to the firm. Hopefully, the subsequent market value weight of the equity component of the package will be much greater. If so, the implication is not that the average cost of funds has changed; the implication is that the cost has been *met*. Since book values measure the relative significance of capital inputs, those are the numbers to use for X_D, X_R, and X_E—even though we must still look to market values to provide an estimate of the discount rate which, given its past investments, investors seem to be applying to our firm now. The latter is an index of the market's probable reaction to future inputs of capital, but the size of the inputs themselves are a separate issue.

7

MEASURING
THE COSTS

Given the conceptual framework described above, the final links in our chain of analysis can now be forged. If our discussion is to be useful to the practicing financial manager, we must provide him with the tools to (1) adapt the approach outlined to an environment in which the earnings and dividends of firms are growing rather than remaining constant over time, and (2) perform the necessary calculations in the context of a more realistic business situation than the examples discussed thus far represent. The latter problem will be addressed by offering an illustrative analysis of a finance "case" where the cost of capital for the corporation involved is the central issue.

DIVIDENDS AND EARNINGS

In examining a firm's capital structure decisions heretofore, we have effectively sidestepped the question as to whether the prospective income stream which investors react to in choosing securities for their portfolios consists of the firm's earnings or its dividends. Our consideration of the debt-equity choice was cast in terms of the two being equal by virtue of assuming full earnings payout. Even in the retained earnings discussion, the distinction was avoided by talking about only a single year's retentions and employing the device of having the individual investor also "retain" a portion of his dividends for reinvestment. While these were legitimate and efficient tactics for constructing a theoretical model, the need to make some cost-of-capital measurements for firms that in practice continually retain earnings and expand precludes any further procrastination. The market capitalization rates which must be estimated for use in our valuation formulas require that we identify precisely which future income stream is pertinent. What, after all, do investors "buy" when they acquire a share of stock?

The answer here[1] is that investors buy the firm's dividends, not its earnings. The intuitive rationale is quite straightforward: dividends constitute the only cash flows produced by the firm for its shareholders and therefore represent the one observable return they receive on their investment. They put up a sum of money to purchase a share of stock—i.e., they forego present consumption—in order to lay claim to a series of subsequent payments that will permit future consumption at a higher level. This trade-off, as perceived by the multitude of individuals who populate the capital markets, is in fact the essence of the community's collective investment decision. Such individuals cannot spend a firm's retained earnings on goods and services; they can spend only the dividends—the *cash* payments—they receive. Retained earnings are not necessarily irrelevant, but they are relevant only insofar as they generate higher *future* dividends. Unless some incremental cash flow eventually occurs, a corporation's retentions have absolutely no value to its stockholders.

As an illustration of this argument, take the case of a firm which has been experiencing annual earnings over a period of years ranging from, say, $4 to $8 per share depending on the general level of economic activity. When the economy is booming, the firm reports earnings near the upper end of that spectrum; in recessions, the lower extreme usually occurs. Despite these fluctuations, however, the firm has paid exactly $3 a share in dividends for the last decade or more and shows no signs of increasing either its dividends or its reported earnings in the foreseeable future. As an investor, am I likely to consider myself purchasing an expected annual income stream of $6—which we shall assume is the figure that earnings average out to over the years—or one of $3? The latter seems the clear choice. Apparently, the only benefit I obtain from the retained earnings is the reliability of my dividend. The firm is on a treadmill, reinvesting at just about the rate which keeps its real earning power constant. It uses what are called "earnings" on its income statement to maintain its plant and equipment, pay its bills to suppliers, and meet its labor costs in such a way that it can afford to part with $3 annually to its

---

[1] And elsewhere in the literature of finance as well. See Myron J. Gordon, *The Investment, Financing, and Valuation of the Corporation* (Homewood, Ill.: Richard D. Irwin, Inc., 1962); Diran Bodenhorn, "On the Problem of Capital Budgeting," *The Journal of Finance,* December 1959, pp. 473–492.

stockholders without losing ground. As far as they are concerned, the $3 is all they can ever expect to receive—despite the fact that the firm's balance sheet indicates it is growing.[2]

CAPITAL GAINS

Statements of this sort must, of course, be made a little more carefully when we recognize that investors do not always acquire stock with the intention of holding it indefinitely. Can the same conclusion be drawn for a securities market in which the participants anticipate capital gains as well as dividends? It can if we attribute the capital gains themselves to the expectation of higher subsequent dividends on the part of the individuals to whom today's shareholders hope eventually to sell their shares. Fortunately, that interpretation does appear legitimate.

Consider the cash income prospects of an individual who purchases a share of stock with the intention of holding it for n years and then reselling it. In return for his immediate outlay of funds, he anticipates a series of annual dividend payments terminating in the resale of the share involved at (hopefully) an increased price. We may therefore tabulate his cash flow projections as follows:

Year	Expected Receipt
1	$\bar{d}_1$
2	$\bar{d}_2$
.	.
.	.
.	.
n	$d_n + \bar{P}_n$

where $\bar{d}_i$ denotes the per-share dividend payment predicted for year i and $\bar{P}_n$ the stock's expected per-share market price at the end of year n.[3] Our investor's decision to acquire this security implies that, in his

[2] Such a situation should not be regarded as an unreasonable or artificial example. There have been—and continue to be—more than a few instances of entire industries whose component firms' earnings and dividends have stagnated for years even while retained earnings were being reported.

[3] The various $\bar{d}_i$'s represent after-corporate-tax payments to shareholders. For convenience, personal taxes will be ignored since their only effect is to lengthen the various expressions involved. The conclusions reached do not depend on either their presence or their absence, as the reader can convince himself by adding taxes as the argument develops.

eyes, the present value of the indicated sequence of cash inflows is equal to or greater than its current market price, P_0. That is

$$P_0 \leqq PV = \sum_{i=1}^{n} \frac{\bar{d}_i}{(1+K)^i} + \frac{\bar{P}_n}{(1+K)^n}, \qquad (7\text{--}1)$$

where K refers to the discount rate which he thinks is appropriate given the uncertainties associated with the various payments.[4]

The question, then, is: On what grounds can our man reasonably hope for this—or any other—set of receipts? Certainly, he will use the firm's past dividend record to predict the relevant $\bar{d}_i$ figures, but what about $\bar{P}_n$? How will he attempt to arrive at an estimate of the stock's potential resale value? The suggestion here is that, if he is a rational man interested in profit opportunities, he will impute the same sort of attitude to other investors. He will assume that anyone who may be interested in buying his stock when he wants to sell it will use a valuation model similar to his own in deciding what the share is worth. Thus, the price $\bar{P}_n$ he foresees can be interpreted as his estimate of the present value he expects the *next* purchaser to place on the stock. Since, to our man, its current present value can be expressed as in equation (7–1) above, he will perceive that $\bar{P}_n$ is just

$$\bar{P}_n = \sum_{i=n+1}^{n+m} \frac{d_i}{(1+K)^{i-n}} + \frac{\bar{P}_{n+m}}{(1+K)^m}, \qquad (7\text{--}2)$$

in which m denotes the number of years he thinks the individual to whom he sells will hold the share in question. Substituting this expression into equation (7–1), we obtain

$$PV = \sum_{i=1}^{n} \frac{\bar{d}_i}{(1+K)^i} + \frac{1}{(1+K)^n} \sum_{i=n+1}^{n+m} \frac{\bar{d}_i}{(1+K)^{i-n}}$$

$$+ \frac{\bar{P}_{n+m}}{(1+K)^n(1+K)^m} \qquad (7\text{--}3)$$

$$PV = \sum_{i=1}^{n+m} \frac{\bar{d}_i}{(1+K)^i} + \frac{\bar{P}_{n+m}}{(1+K)^{n+m}} \qquad (7\text{--}4)$$

[4] K is adopted as the notation for this rate because, as we shall see, it turns out to be conceptually the same K which was defined in Chapter 4, equation (4–45). See pp. 47–48.

as an expanded statement of our current shareholder's valuation formula. He must—if only implicitly—predict the dividends and the capital gain his successor can expect if he is to come to a meaningful conclusion about the possible size of his own capital gain.

But what of $\overline{P}_{n+m}$? We cannot really say much about $\overline{P}_n$ unless we consider the price the second investor in the chain is likely to predict for *his* resale transaction. What will the third man be apt to pay?[5] Well, if we assume that man number 2 performs something akin to a present value analysis, the same should be true of man number 3. Accordingly, we may write

$$\overline{P}_{n+m} = \sum_{i=n+m+1}^{n+m+q} \frac{d_i}{(1+K)^{i-n-m}} + \frac{\overline{P}_{n+m+q}}{(1+K)^q}, \qquad (7\text{-}5)$$

q denoting the expected holding period for the third man. Thus

$$PV = \sum_{i=1}^{n+m} \frac{d_i}{(1+K)^i} + \frac{1}{(1+K)^{n+m}} \sum_{i=n+m+1}^{n+m+q} \frac{d_i}{(1+K)^{i-n-m}}$$
$$+ \frac{\overline{P}_{n+m+q}}{(1+K)^{n+m}(1+K)^q} \qquad (7\text{-}6)$$

$$PV = \sum_{i=1}^{n+m+q} \frac{d_i}{(1+k)^i} + \frac{\overline{P}_{n+m+q}}{(1+K)^{n+m+q}}, \qquad (7\text{-}7)$$

and we thereupon restate the worth of a share of stock today as the present value of a stream of dividends $n + m + q$ years long plus the present value of its market price at the end of that interval.

It should not be necessary to carry the game further to make the intended point. If we keep repeating this process—which in principle we should do in order to predict the successive $\overline{P}_i$'s—we eventually reach a situation in which the formula for PV is an infinite stream of (presumably growing) discounted dividend payments and the last relevant resale price is indefinitely far in the future. Indeed, once we get past 25 or 30 years of inflows in such an analysis, the subsequent dividends as well as that ultimate price can be ignored because, for any meaningful discount rate K, they add virtually nothing to our estimate of PV.[6] As a result, we end up with an expression for the

[5] These so-called "men" obviously are stand-ins for the consensus of the entire market about future stock prices.
[6] For example, the present value of $1 a year for 30 years at a 10 percent discount rate is $9.43. The present value of $1 a year in perpetuity is $10.

worth of a share of stock in a world where investors actively seek capital gains, which is paradoxically nothing more than the present value of the firm's per-share dividend payments during the foreseeable future. It is incontrovertible that the only thing investors receive in return for purchasing securities is a series of dividend payments plus a terminal capital gain. All we need accept is this almost tautological view of the securities market and the conclusion above follows automatically. Investors in fact "buy" dividends. Their capital gains are merely the product of anticipated higher future dividends.[7]

A final note. Since the implication is that the valuation process described will be going on continually throughout the market in connection with all securities traded, we may specify

$$P_0 = PV \qquad (7\text{--}8)$$

as an equilibrium condition. The opinions of every investor about the value of any shares available for purchase will lead to a set of observable prices. If even one individual believes the share of stock we have been talking about is undervalued at its existing price, he will be led to add it to his portfolio and thereby push up its price until equation (7–8) is satisfied. In this respect, our present-value-of-dividends model is both a statement of individual attitudes *and* a market valuation formula.

NON-DIVIDEND-PAYING SHARES

The argument that investors react basically to a firm's dividend prospects can be extended to situations in which no dividends are being paid at the moment simply by asserting that investors are willing to acquire the shares of such firms in the expectation that payments eventually *will* be forthcoming. Today's stock purchaser may or may not anticipate any dividend receipts during the interval he intends to hold the shares at issue, but his hope of enjoying a

---

[7] The reader may feel that there must have been a little sleight-of-hand involved in the preceding analysis—and, indeed, the whole process does look somewhat like pulling a rabbit out of a hat. The only real qualification necessary, however, concerns the rate of growth projected for the firm's dividends and stock price over time. The argument made about ignoring both past a certain point because in present value terms they become negligible is appropriate as long as neither is growing at an annual rate greater than K. This seems a reasonable assumption if for no other reason than the fact that if it were not true, the current price of the firm's stock would be infinite—and there are not very many shares traded in that range in the market even among "glamour" stocks. See also below, p. 96.

terminal capital gain must necessarily rest on the belief that the market does expect payments to begin at some point. In the context of the previous section, there must be a series of positive $\bar{d}_i$ values predicted somewhere along the way if P_0 is to be positive. The question may be posed: Would a rational investor be willing to buy a share of stock in a firm whose corporate charter forbade it ever to pay a dividend? The answer that he might if he expected a capital gain is no answer at all. He can count on such a gain only if he has some logical grounds for believing that another investor will be attracted to the same share later on—and if no cash flows are ever to be produced by the firm for its owners, there is no reason for anyone to be interested in acquiring its stock at any time. The firm will be a steady absorber of funds from the rest of the business community. One supposes that it will eventually explode under the pressure of holding too many assets—or, like a dinosaur, will perish of its own sheer bulk. Speculation about the nature of these possible outcomes, however, is perhaps of secondary concern here.[8]

DIVIDEND GROWTH AND DIVIDEND YIELD

If we can agree, then, that dividends constitute the relevant income stream for shareholders, we can return to the basic measurement equation developed earlier and proceed to modify it to take corporate growth into account. We found that for a levered firm in a tax environment, the relationship between the dividend yield on its common stock, the market capitalization rate for unlevered firms in its risk class, the market price of its stock, and the amount of its outstanding long-term debt could be expressed as[9]

$$K = \alpha_t + (\alpha_t - r)(1 - t_c)\left(\frac{D}{V_S}\right). \qquad (7\text{--}9)$$

Our objective is to insert available market data into this formula in order to compute the α_t which belongs in our cost of capital equations.

Now, as long as a corporation is assumed to be paying out all its earnings as dividends and not expanding, K represents *both* a dividend yield and an earnings-price ratio. In either case, it has the dimensions of a percentage figure and denotes in effect the discount

---

[8] The point that investors might buy shares in such a firm in order to gain voting control and liquidate it only serves to reinforce the argument presented. The act of liquidation is of interest because it in fact *does* give rise to a cash flow—an ultimate "dividend."

[9] See again pp. 47–48.

rate the market is applying to the firm's expected future income net of interest charges and corporate taxes. It is therefore exactly the same sort of discount rate we have just been talking about. Given the risk class to which the firm belongs and the capital structure it has chosen, investors will respond by using the rate K to appraise its per-share income prospects and arrive at a price for its stock. In a situation where those prospects are for a level annual dividend and earnings stream, we have simply

$$P_0 = \sum_{i=1}^{\infty} \frac{\bar{d}}{(1+K)^i} = \frac{\bar{d}}{K}, \tag{7-10}$$

where $\bar{d}$ refers to expected annual per-share income and P_0 is today's stock price. For purposes of equation (7-9), we can find K from the observable ratio $\bar{d}/P_0$ and go on to solve for α_t as indicated in Chapter 4.[10]

When dividends and earnings are not equal, however, and we recognize that both will grow as a result of the firm's reinvestment of retained earnings, we reach two important conclusions: (1) that dividends are the item to be discounted rather than earnings; and (2) that the ratio of the current year's dividend to today's stock price is no longer a meaningful estimate of K. Investors clearly are not using a 2 percent discount rate in deciding that a firm whose existing dividend is $1 per share should be worth $50—a relationship which has not been uncommon in the market in recent years. They are, of course, projecting a rise in future dividends and arriving at $50 as the present value of some increasing series of cash payments. Accordingly, our problem is to determine the K which applies to "growth" stocks.

Put formally, the discount rate we seek is the one that satisfies the equation

$$P_0 = \sum_{i=1}^{\infty} \frac{\bar{d}_i}{(1+K)^i}, \tag{7-11}$$

in which the expectation is, for all i,

$$\bar{d}_{i+1} > \bar{d}_i. \tag{7-12}$$

If the firm's dividends have been growing in past years at the annual rate g and we have reason to believe this trend will continue, we may express each anticipated future dividend payment as

$$\bar{d}_i = d_0(1+g)^i. \tag{7-13}$$

[10] Pp. 48–50.

That is, the payment predicted for year i will be equal to the dividend the firm *actually* paid during the most recent year for which data are available, d_0, multiplied by the compound growth factor $(1 + g)^i$. For example, the dividend in the coming year—year 1—will be expected to be $(1 + g)$ times as large as last year's payment, that expected in the following year $(1 + g)^2$ times as large, and so on.

This approach will be both acceptable and useful as long as the firm's growth is expected to be fairly steady and approximate the annual rate g in the long run despite possible short-term fluctuations. If the historical value for g is suspect because of some recent change in the firm's circumstances, our interest is in discovering the figure which the market now thinks is relevant. A quick survey of investment bankers, stock brokerage firms' newsletters, and investment advisory services' publications should give us a pretty good estimate. The question is: What predictions are being made by those people whose business it is to advise investors whether to buy or sell our stock and whose attitudes therefore have created the P_0 we observe? Certainly, our firm's historical growth record is likely to provide the basis for most such predictions and is a logical place to begin.

Having decided on a value for g, we can readily determine the K it implies. Substituting for $\bar{d}_i$ in equation (7–11), we have

$$P_0 = \sum_{i=1}^{\infty} \frac{d_0(1 + g)^i}{(1 + K)^i} = d_0 \sum_{i=1}^{\infty} \left(\frac{1 + g}{1 + K} \right) \cdot \qquad (7\text{–}14)$$

Since we have established that

$$\sum_{i=1}^{\infty} \left(\frac{1}{1 + x} \right)^i = \frac{1}{x} \qquad (7\text{–}15)$$

for any positive x, we may define

$$\frac{1 + g}{1 + K} = \frac{1}{1 + x}, \qquad (7\text{–}16)$$

which means that[11]

[11] The implicit requirement here is that g be less than K. Otherwise, the x defined will be negative and the infinite series represented by equation (7–15) will literally sum to infinity rather than to $1/x$. A similar point was raised above on p. 93, the conclusion simply being that the market will always end up using a sufficiently high K that no firm will ever command an infinite price for its stock, regardless of the pace of its growth. For a related discussion, see David Durand, "Growth Stocks and the Petersburg Paradox," *The Journal of Finance*, September 1957, pp. 348–363.

$$x = \frac{K - g}{1 + g}. \tag{7-17}$$

Therefore, our expression for P_0 becomes

$$P_0 = d_0\left(\frac{1}{x}\right) = \frac{d_0(1 + g)}{K - g}, \tag{7-18}$$

and, solving for K,

$$K = \frac{d_0(1 + g)}{P_0} + g. \tag{7-19}$$

Now, the term $d_0(1 + g)$ represents just the per-share dividend expected during year 1, $\bar{d}_1$. We may thereupon write as our final expression for K

$$K = \frac{\bar{d}_1}{P_0} + g. \tag{7-20}$$

The discount rate the investment community seems to be applying to our firm's future dividend stream is equal to the ratio of the coming year's anticipated dividend to our current stock price *plus* the annual rate at which dividends are expected to grow. This, by definition, is the after-corporate-tax capitalization rate which has produced P_0 and can be interpreted as the "growth-adjusted" dividend yield for our firm. More importantly at the moment, it is precisely the value for K we want in equation (7–9) in order to calculate α_t. Equation (7–20) modifies our underlying valuation model to take corporate growth into account; equation (7–9) places that adjustment in the context of the firm's debt-equity ratio and specifies the relationship between the various financial parameters which should hold in a tax environment. As a result, we now have all the equipment we need to determine a firm's cost of capital.

COMMENTARY

Two brief observations about equation (7–20) are in order. We may note that if the firm's dividends are not expected to grow—i.e., g is equal to zero—we simply return to the situation of Chapter 4 as summarized by equation (7–10) above. K can be estimated as the ratio of the coming year's dividend to today's stock price because all the future $\bar{d}_i$'s are the same.

The other point concerns the sensitivity of our estimate of K to stock price fluctuations. Since there will always be some imprecision in our analysis due to the difficulties involved in making predictions and appraising investors' attitudes, it would be nice to feel that the answers we get are not too sensitive to alternative assumptions about certain of the data inputs. Clearly, the figure we obtain for K will depend heavily on our estimate of g—but fortunately it will *not* depend much on P_0 for a growing company. Even fairly severe day-to-day or week-to-week changes in the firm's stock price during the time when we are attempting to calculate its cost of capital and decide on what sort of funds to raise will have little impact on K as long as a reasonable rate of dividend growth is expected.

For example, if the projected growth rate is 10 percent per annum and the dividend payment anticipated for the coming year is $1, it will make only a minor difference to our computations whether the firm's shares are selling for $40, $50, or $60 currently. The three values of K we would end up with are

$$K_1 = \frac{\$1}{\$40} + .10 = 12.5 \text{ percent} \tag{7-21}$$

$$K_2 = \frac{\$1}{\$50} + .10 = 12.0 \text{ percent} \tag{7-22}$$

$$K_3 = \frac{\$1}{\$60} + .10 = 11.7 \text{ percent.} \tag{7-23}$$

Similar results would emerge for other sets of assumptions. Because we will have a substantial body of historical data on which to base our estimate of g, we are likely to have more confidence in that figure than in the fact that today's stock price reflects only a sober appraisal by the market of our long-run financing strategy and investment decisions and is therefore devoid of the influence of short-term external economic factors. It is therefore encouraging to find that K will not vary significantly depending on which day of the month we happen to pick a P_0 to use in our equations.

A CASE PROBLEM

Let us turn, then, to an application of the model. Consider the following hypothetical situation:

The Apex Appliance Corporation

The Apex Appliance Corporation is a medium-sized manufacturer of electrical household appliances. Its product line ranges from items as small as electric toothbrushes and can openers up to window fans and vacuum cleaners. The company is organized into several divisions, generally according to product types. Its appliances are sold nationally, the firm's brand name being an important element in its sales effort.

During the late 1950s and early 1960s, sales and earnings grew quite rapidly. Sales in 1956 were approximately $60 million, but had reached $180 million by 1966. Per-share earnings and dividends more than kept pace. The relevant figures are tabulated in Exhibit A. Because the company depends on the family as its customer unit—and because many of its products can be classified as luxury items—its year-to-year operating results are somewhat affected by overall economic conditions. Sales and profits therefore fluctuate cyclically around whatever longer-term pattern occurs.

In order to support the firm's expansion, substantial expenditures on plant and equipment were required during the period indicated. The majority of the funds came from retained earnings and the private placement of debentures with insurance companies. In 1959, however, the company was forced to sell additional common stock because it felt that the debt level which would ensue from trying to borrow the money to keep up with its expansion program would be excessive. In particular, possible adverse effects on its stock price were feared since, at the time, the company's ratio of debt to total capitalization was already somewhat above the industry average of 30 percent. The firm's balance sheet as of December 31, 1966, is shown in Exhibit B.

Originally, the company's board of directors had established a policy of paying out half its annual earnings as dividends. The actual percentage varied from year to year because an attempt was made to stabilize the dividend despite fluctuating profits. By the late 1950s, however, this policy had been revised to set one-third of earnings as the target figure due to the continuing need for new capital. At their last meeting, the directors announced that the 1967 dividend rate would be 60 cents per share, payable in quarterly installments of 15 cents. The company's stock is listed on a major securities exchange and actively traded. The range of yearly prices is included in Exhibit A. The closing price on January 15, 1967, was $30.

EXHIBIT A.   *Operating results and financial data, 1956–1966.*

Year	Sales, in Millions	Earnings Per Share*	Dividends Per Share*	Stock Price Range*
1956	$ 60	$ .56	$.30	$ 6–10
1957	63	.50	.30	5–9
1958	68	.71	.35	5–10
1959	85	.88	.40	8–12
1960	97	.82	.45	9–14
1961	119	.94	.45	12–20
1962	130	1.11	.45	11–18
1963	145	1.35	.45	15–24
1964	164	1.36	.50	17–27
1965	173	1.60	.50	20–30
1966	180	1.75	.60	24–32

* Adjusted for 3:1 stock split in 1959.

Early in 1967, the treasurer of Apex was reviewing its investment and financing strategies with an eye toward improving both. The question as to the appropriate cut-off rate of return on new investments was of special concern. The treasurer was of the opinion that many capital expenditures had been made in the past without proper analysis. He wanted a figure that could be justified to the company's several divisional managers as its cost of capital in order that he might achieve more uniform and accurate capital budgeting procedures throughout the organization.

EXHIBIT B.   *Balance sheet, 12/31/66 (figures in millions).*

Assets

Cash	$ 20
Accounts receivable	10
Inventories	30
Plant and equipment, net	60
Total	$120

Liabilities and Net Worth

Current liabilities	$ 40
Long-term debt*	24
Common stock (2.5 million shares)	16
Retained earnings	40
Total	$120

*Interest charges amounted to $1.08 million in 1966.

ANALYSIS

While the foregoing is obviously a rather cryptic description of the firm's circumstances and history, it does contain all the elements essential to a cost of capital calculation. We can observe that the company's earnings per share have been growing at an annual rate of 12 percent during the last decade. That is, in the relationship

$$(1956 \; EPS)(1 + g)^{10} = (1966 \; EPS) \qquad (7\text{--}24)$$

$$(\$.56)(1 + g)^{10} = (\$1.75), \qquad (7\text{--}25)$$

we find that g is equal to 12 percent. This growth has been subject to cyclical influences, but the long-run trend appears fairly stable and the departures from it not too extreme. Figure 7–1 illustrates the point. If it seems reasonable to believe that this pattern will continue—or, more accurately, if it seems likely the investment community holds that opinion—the resulting g is the figure we want for our calculations.

FIGURE 7–1. *Apex appliance earnings per share.*

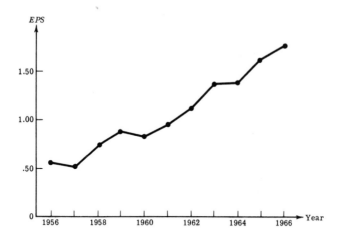

This conclusion may appear to contradict the statements made above to the effect that it is the expected dividend growth rate which is of interest in connection with stock valuation. In fact, the position here remains that dividends *are* the relevant item—but in the Apex case our estimate of *g* is most appropriately obtained indirectly. Since the firm reduced its target dividend payout ratio during the time period for which we have data, the observed historical dividend rate of growth is apt to be misleading as a basis for extrapolation. It will understate the pace at which dividends should grow in subsequent years if the firm hereafter maintains its new target payout ratio of one-third of annual earnings.[12] In effect, the argument is that the rate of growth of past earnings is in this instance a better guide to the probable rate of growth of future dividends than is the historical trend of dividends themselves. The *g* we are concerned with is always a dividend *g*—but the recent dividend record of the firm may not always be our best source of information.[13]

If we can assume, then, that the investing public anticipates a 12 percent annual increase in the Apex Corporation's per-share dividend over the long run, it must be true that a discount rate of

[12] Clearly, this latter assumption is crucial—and we must feel that investors believe it.

[13] In all cases, the pertinent figures are *per-share* earnings and dividends since the individual investor's circumstances are at issue. Any stock splits or stock dividends by the firm must therefore be taken into account in compiling the historical growth pattern for one of today's shares.

$$K = \frac{d_i}{P_0} + g = \frac{\$.60}{\$30} + .12 = 14 \text{ percent} \qquad (7\text{–}26)$$

is being used to evaluate that growing stream of payments. This is the only figure that can explain the $30 share price we now see quoted for the firm's stock in the market. Given this evidence, the implied cost of capital is easily computed.

The firm's long-term debt amounts to $24 million.[14] The average rate of interest paid is 4.5 percent, which we can infer from the total annual interest charges of $1.08 million noted in Exhibit B. The aggregate market value of Apex common stock is $75 million—2.5 million shares at $30 each. Thus, we have

$$K = \alpha_t + (\alpha_t - r)(1 - t_c)\left(\frac{D}{V_S}\right) \qquad (7\text{–}9)$$

$$.14 = \alpha_t + (\alpha_t - .045)(1 - .50)\left(\frac{\$24}{\$75}\right), \qquad (7\text{–}27)$$

from which we determine that α_t is equal to 12.7 percent. This figure represents, according to our underlying model, the market capitalization rate for unlevered firms in the "risk class" to which Apex Appliance belongs. It implies that the cost to the company of the three forms of capital it has been employing are

$$R_E = \frac{\alpha_t}{1 - b} = \frac{.127}{1 - .10} = 14.1 \text{ percent} \qquad (7\text{–}28)$$

$$R_R = \alpha_t \frac{(1 - t_p)}{(1 - t_g)} = \frac{(.127)(1 - .30)}{(1 - .10)} = 10.0 \text{ percent} \qquad (7\text{–}29)$$

$$R_D = \alpha_t (1 - t_c) = (.127)(1 - .50) = 6.4 \text{ percent} \qquad (7\text{–}30)$$

on the assumption that the firm typically receives 10 percent less than the prevailing market price of its stock from a new issue due to underwriting expenses and underpricing. The capital gains and personal income tax rates suggested in Chapter 5 are adopted as the relevant ones for Apex stockholders.[15]

The company has in the past raised 30 percent of its long-term funds by borrowing—$24 million of the total long-term capitalization

[14] Assuming that its book value and current market value are the same. If they differ, market value is the required figure at the moment.
[15] See pp. 72–74.

of $80 million shown on its balance sheet. Retained earnings have provided $40 million and common stock issues the remaining $16 million. Book value figures are used in this connection because, as discussed earlier, we want a measure of the relative importance of the various capital *input*s to the firm in order to talk about their costs.[16] If we believe the company will maintain the indicated set of proportions in its capital structure over time, we have

$$X_E = \$16/\$80 = .20 \qquad (7\text{--}31)$$

$$X_R = \$40/\$80 = .50 \qquad (7\text{--}32)$$

$$X_D = \$24/\$80 = .30, \qquad (7\text{--}33)$$

and its weighted average after-tax cost of capital is simply

$$R_A = (X_E)(R_E) + (X_R)(R_R) + (X_D)(R_D) \qquad (7\text{--}34)$$

$$R_A = (.2)(.141) + (.5)(.10) + (.3)(.064) \qquad (7\text{--}35)$$

$$R_A = 9.7 \text{ percent.} \qquad (7\text{--}36)$$

The company should use this figure to compute the after-tax present value of any investments it contemplates which expand its appliance manufacturing activities—or, alternatively, should reject any such projects that do not promise a higher expected after-tax rate of return.

It may be noted that, if the directors of Apex should adopt a policy of not going to the capital markets to issue common stock in the future and thereby limit investments to those which can be financed out of retained earnings and increased borrowing, the firm's average cost of *new* capital would no longer be 9.7 percent. The figure would become instead

$$R_A = (X_R)(R_R) + (X_D)(R_D) \qquad (7\text{--}37)$$

$$R_A = (.70)(.10) + (.30)(.064) \qquad (7\text{--}38)$$

$$R_A = 8.9 \text{ percent} \qquad (7\text{--}39)$$

as long as 30 percent of the total continued to come from borrowing. Thus, the historical R_A is the correct figure to use in appraising future investments *if* the historical capital structure is to be maintained

---

[16] Pp. 86–87.

as the firm grows. If not, the average cost of the new set of capital proportions is the number we want. Another way of stating the same proposition is to observe that, if the firm's finance mix changes, its long-run average and marginal costs of capital will differ.

ACCURACY OF THE ANALYSIS

The case described is, of course, a rather more convenient one to analyze than most business situations will be. The data included were designed to generate a clear-cut set of answers and to remove much of the ambiguity that often confronts the practicing financial manager. From his standpoint, satisfactory estimates of g, α_t, and R_A are likely to be somewhat harder to come by. His firm's dividend and earnings record may well be more erratic and his confidence in being able to interpret investors' reactions less pervasive. The contention here, however, is that the philosophy and the approach he should employ are as outlined above—and that, despite the difficulties he will encounter, better decisions are apt to be made with the right conceptual framework in mind than the wrong one. Several estimates of the firm's cost of capital based on different assumptions about the various input quantities may be necessary in many instances. As long as those estimates are not terribly sensitive to changes in such assumptions, a major piece of information for improving the firm's financial strategies will have been obtained. While we cannot offer a neat formula which will replace an experienced financial manager's judgment, we can attempt to improve the data with which he works and illuminate the possible consequences of the alternatives he faces. If the present volume accomplishes nothing more than that, its objectives will have been met.

OTHER RISK CLASSES

A final point concerns the relevance of the figure we obtain for R_A to investments the firm may be considering that are not of the same general type as its existing operations. Corporations often come across opportunities to diversify or to expand "vertically" and thereby to make capital expenditures in what would be termed here other "risk classes." In evaluating such opportunities, the cost of capital determined for the firm as presently constituted is not really the one that should be used. The appropriate figure instead is the cost of capital which seems indicated for other firms that are already in the line of business being examined. For example, a tobacco company which is contemplating the acquisition of a food processor should employ in its appraisal the cost of capital that food processing firms appear to experience rather than the tobacco industry figure. Unless the profits anticipated from the acquisition, when discounted at the food processing capital cost, have a present value greater than the price to be paid for them, the purchase is unwise. The implication therefore is that there may be several "costs of capital" the firm should take into account in a given year in drawing up its capital budget, depending on how significantly the investment projects being considered differ from its existing activities. In every case, an investment must pass the same test that others like it—others which are as risky—pass elsewhere in the economy if it is to be acceptable.

It should be emphasized in this connection that our interest lies in determining the α_t value that applies to a project and then using *that* number to calculate the associated R_A, just as we did above. The latter parameter may not necessarily be the same R_A confronted by firms that are currently engaged in projects of the type being evaluated. α_t is our basic measure of the market's attitude toward a risk class of investments. R_A, however, is a function of corporations' capital structure decisions as well. Every firm in a particular industry may have a different average cost of capital 'because of differing financial strategies, even though the asset investments and pre-tax earnings prospects of each company are similar. In terms of the example offered, we would say that if our tobacco company's capital structure differs from that of most food processors, the appropriate procedure would be to attempt to estimate the α_t applicable to food processing— by techniques of the sort described for the Apex Appliance case—and then to use the tobacco company's X_D, X_R, and X_E in calculating the R_A it should employ in appraising the proposed acquisition.

If a firm has a large number of investments to consider, many of which seem to be not precisely like its current ones, it is clear that the task of finding the "correct" set of capital costs can become onerous. One way to simplify the problem would be to separate the various projects into a limited number of standard categories and to choose a single R_A for each category. Thus, a company which estimated that the average cost of capital associated with its existing line of business was 10 percent might arbitrarily specify 5 percent as the discount rate for projects considered significantly "less risky" and 15 percent for those significantly "more risky." While the majority of its investments would almost assuredly be placed in the middle category, a not unreasonable distinction between proposals based on the perceived degree of profit uncertainty connected with each would be achieved. The design and implementation of such a scheme are properly the concern of a capital budgeting text, however.[17] The important point here is that any arrangement of this sort has as its rationale the fact that investments with different characteristics are viewed by the market in a manner which suggests that not one but *several* "costs of capital"—required rates of return—may well be pertinent to a corporation's decisions.

EPILOGUE

This chapter therefore pretty well completes the cycle which was begun in Chapter 2. A conceptual framework for identifying capital costs in an uncertain world has been developed and the techniques necessary to apply that framework outlined. While there is no claim that either aspect of the problem has been "solved" in a way that is likely to make the reader completely comfortable with the recommendations offered, the hope is that the analysis will at least contribute to that solution when it eventually comes—and that it may improve the decision-making process in the meantime.

[17] See Robert W. Johnson, *Capital Budgeting* (Belmont, Calif.: Wadsworth Publishing Company, Inc.). A related analysis which explores the assumptions about uncertainty that are implicit in this approach can be found in Alexander A. Robichek and Stewart C. Myers, *Optimal Financing Decisions* (Englewood Cliffs, N.J.: Prentice-Hall, Inc., 1965), pp. 67–93.

8

RELATED FINANCIAL
CONSIDERATIONS

There are a number of issues closely related to the question of a firm's cost of capital and to the validity of the model described above which, either explicitly or implicitly, have been sidestepped thus far. Even though none of these alters the conclusions drawn from the analysis, several are sufficiently important to merit attention in the interest of comprehensiveness.

PORTFOLIO MANAGEMENT

The focus of our discussion throughout has been an examination of the income prospects of the individual shareholder and of the manner in which those prospects are affected by the corporation's capital structure decisions. Since we began by tying the analysis to an investor's utility-of-wealth perceptions, the mean and the variance of future income streams have been of particular concern. It should be pointed out, however, that in a broader conceptual framework the process of making comparisons between the shares of firms on the basis of those characteristic parameters is not quite as self-contained as it has been made to appear here.

The real problem in appraising the attractiveness of a given security to a potential purchaser lies in determining how the income stream associated with the security fits into his total portfolio of investments. Thus, the relevant question is not simply: What are the mean and variance of the prospective income stream involved? The question is instead: How do that mean and variance affect the mean and variance of the investor's *aggregate* income?

Consider the stocks of two firms, A and B, each of whose probability distribution of annual per-share earnings and dividends is:

Possible Dividend	Probability
$2	$\frac{1}{2}$
0	$\frac{1}{2}$

While in these terms the shares of the two firms would seem to present equivalent opportunities and might be expected to be equally attractive to investors, it is not difficult to conceive of circumstances in which this will not be the case at all. Suppose we look at the two through the eyes of an individual whose entire securities portfolio consists at the moment of one share of stock in firm C. The latter company's probability distribution of earnings and dividends is exactly like those of firms A and B—with one very significant additional feature: Firm C always has its good and bad years *simultaneously* with firm A but *opposite* to firm B. That is, every time firm A earns $2 per share, so does firm C, while firm B earns nothing; when firm B makes a $2 profit, the other two just break even. An investor who owns a share in firm C therefore can count on receiving precisely $2 every year if he adds one B share to his portfolio, but if he buys an A share, his prospective annual dividend receipts will be described by the probability distribution:

Possible Receipt	Probability
$4	$\frac{1}{2}$
0	$\frac{1}{2}$

Clearly, the two alternatives are not identical. According to the arguments made in Chapter 2 about risk aversion, we would expect our man to prefer the stock of firm B as his next security purchase.

The situation need not be cast in such strong terms in order to make the point, however. *Any* interdependence between investment outcomes is of concern to shareholders, and comparisons between firms A and B of the kind which have been presented throughout our discussion cannot really be undertaken in a vacuum. Not only must the characteristics of the two income streams at issue be considered, but so must their relationship to the rest of investors' portfolios. This suggests, in effect, that the definition above of a "risk class" to which two firms belong as a device to permit a comparative analysis of their financial policies has built into it one of three implicit assumptions:

1. That there is literally no interdependence between the operating results of firms in that risk class and those of other corporations in the economy.
2. That any such interdependence is sufficiently mild that it can be ignored for all practical purposes.

3. That the interdependence is of roughly the same order of magnitude for all firms in the risk class and therefore the stock of each is an acceptable substitute for any others in a given portfolio.

Only if one of these conditions is met will it be legitimate to concentrate as we have on the risk class itself to the exclusion of broader portfolio management considerations. The last of the three has perhaps the most intuitive appeal as a basis for argument. If we think of a group of firms in a particular industry as the most likely example of a risk class, the third assumption above is equivalent to asserting that the profits of all such companies will be affected to about the same extent by changes in economic conditions outside the industry. That should not be too unreasonable an expectation under most sets of circumstances. The full implications of the portfolio management problem for financial decisions, however, require a volume of their own and can only be hinted at here.[1]

THE SECURITIES MARKET

Apart from the question as to how various securities fit together in a total investment package, an assumption about the underlying behavior pattern of individual investors has also been woven into our discussion. In examining shareholders' reactions to alternative capital structure choices by corporations, we have attributed to them a complete lack of prejudice about such choices and complete objectivity in exploring possible offsetting or complementary strategies of their own. Investors have been regarded as acting in what might loosely be termed a "rational" manner. They are assumed to thoroughly investigate and carefully appraise a firm's dividend and earnings prospects and then to ask themselves whether they might lay claim to the same sort of potential returns by appropriate manipulation of their personal finances—including borrowing on personal account. The conclusion throughout has been that the presence or absence of equivalent opportunities elsewhere will determine the extent to which a given corporation's share price will be affected by its leverage and dividend policies.

Obviously, this view of the world places a rather heavy burden not

---

[1] The pioneering work in this area was done by Harry Markowitz in "Portfolio Selection," *Journal of Finance*, March 1952, pp. 77–91. A recent extension of the analytical procedures can be found in William F. Sharpe, "A Simplified Model for Portfolio Analysis," *Management Science*, January 1963, pp. 277–293.

only on our faith in investors' competence and maturity but on the efficiency of the capital markets in general. We must believe, in effect, that the whole system works pretty much in the manner the economic textbooks describe: Reasonable men making informed decisions in an orderly environment. Can such an assumption be maintained?

The contention here is that, in the long run at least, it can. For one thing, the marketplace in question has many of the characteristics of the classical model of "pure competition." Securities are traded by a multitude of economic units, no single one of which is a significant factor in relation to aggregate supply and demand. By and large, each must take the existing price of the commodity traded as given and none can really affect that price very much as a result of its own activities. Entry to and exit from the market are entirely unimpeded. Transactions costs are quite small in comparison with the size of a typical purchase. Information flows freely among both buyers and sellers.[2] While in the short run there may well be considerable "noise" and some friction present in the prices we see quoted, most of the important prerequisites for an efficient long-run performance do exist.

The other condition—that the participants in the market be rational —is also less outrageous an hypothesis than it might at first appear. There is a very strong incentive for investors to behave logically and analyze securities carefully even if logic and thoroughness are not necessarily native character traits. That incentive, of course, is simply greed—or, phrased more conventionally, the "profit motive." It is to an investor's continual advantage to identify differential opportunities to make money, to seek a realistic appraisal of the relative worth of various shares of stock, and to search for alternatives not yet recognized by other investors. Indeed, there exists a considerable population of professional security analysts who make their living by doing just that and selling the resulting information to the less informed. It does not take very many of these clever traders to create a framework in which sensible (rational) prices for securities will tend to be approached and thereby to form the underlying structure around which any short-term fluctuations will occur. An incorrect assessment of a firm's prospects should not persist for too long in the presence of a substantial body of experts who are always on the lookout for someone else's mistakes. In effect, the argument is that, as familiarity breeds contempt, avarice breeds rationality—and avarice *is* a charac-

---

[2] Albeit with a time lag that seems to favor certain "insiders."

ter trait which can be counted on to endure. This contention is the basis for the corollary proposition that the model of the security valuation process described in the preceding chapters is an acceptable one if it is viewed as a statement primarily about long-run relationships. A firm clearly is less likely to affect its share price in the short run by its capital structure decisions alone.

DIVIDENDS AND STOCK REPURCHASES

Such broad matters of philosophy and concept are not the only topics which deserve rather more attention than they were given above, however. There is a series of quite specific issues concerning a corporation's financial strategies that remain to be considered. Among these is the question of the relative desirability of cash dividends to shareholders and repurchases by the firm of its own stock in the market.

The point was made in Chapter 6 that a company may well find itself in a position where it has more funds available for reinvestment in a particular year than it has investment opportunities that promise rates of return exceeding its cost of capital.[3] The suggestion was that those funds be released to stockholders as long as the firm anticipates no shortage of capital for forthcoming profitable investments in subsequent years. While the obvious way to accomplish that objective would be to pay a higher cash dividend than normal, our current federal tax structure renders this policy less efficient than one of having the firm instead use its excess cash to repurchase and retire shares of its stock. In the latter case, shareholders are subject only to a capital gains tax on their participation in the outflow of funds from the firm,[4] whereas they must pay the full ordinary personal income tax rate on any cash dividend receipts.

The argument is reinforced by the market's affection for a stable or steadily growing cash dividend. If a firm's dividend payout is increased—even though that increase is identified by management as a "special" occurrence rather than a permanent adjustment—investors have a way of being upset when something similar does not appear in

---

[3] See pp. 81–83.

[4] This participation takes the form of a capital gain because the number of shares outstanding are reduced by the expenditure of the excess cash with no offsetting reduction in the firm's earning power. As a result, the immediate price increase produced by the entry of the firm on the demand side of the market for its stock should persist even after buying ceases due to the higher per-share income prospects of the remaining shares.

the following year. Stock repurchases, on the other hand, can be executed without fanfare and terminated without any loss of good-will.[5] Corporations which consider their excess cash position to be a temporary phenomenon may therefore find stock retirement a more flexible outlet for funds as well as more desirable from a tax stand-point.

If all of this makes sense, of course, the logical conclusion is that a firm should never pay a cash dividend but should always use stock retirement as its vehicle to generate cash flows to shareholders. Now, that is not really the recommendation here even though it does have considerable theoretical appeal. One of the problems is that the tax advantage sought can be pretty well wiped out for small shareholders in low marginal tax brackets by the brokerage fees—and inconven-ience—associated with selling off a few shares each year to realize the cash flow that dividends would otherwise provide. And some investors simply do like to have a regular cash income. Perhaps a more telling long-run objection, however, has to do with political realities. If a great many corporations adopted such a policy for tax reasons, it is almost certain that the federal government would act to close the resulting tax "loophole" by interpreting most stock repurchase trans-actions as equivalent to dividend payments, thereby denying them capital gains treatment. Nonetheless, for a given firm with a tempo-rary surplus of cash, stock retirement has much to recommend it. Recent evidence in fact suggests that this attitude is becoming increas-ingly accepted in practice.[6]

A final comment concerns the implications of these arguments for a corporation's cost of capital. If it *were* possible for the firm to put its shareholders in a position where all their income was taxed at capital gains rates, we would conclude that the cost of retained earn-ings would be exactly equal to the capitalization rate α_t which defines the firm's "risk class." Thus, we saw above that the required rate of return on investments financed by retentions could be expressed as

$$R_R = \alpha_t \frac{(1 - t_p)}{(1 - t_g)}, \tag{5-45}$$

---

[5] Our interest in the market's "goodwill," it should be emphasized, is a function of our concern with preventing declines in the price of the company's stock.

[6] See, for example L. A. Guthart, "More Companies Are Buying Back Their Own Stock," *Harvard Business Review,* March–April 1965, pp. 40–53, and C. D. Ellis, "Repurchase Stock to Revitalize Equity," *Harvard Business Re-view,* July–August 1965, pp. 119–128.

where t_p is the personal income tax rate on dividend receipts and t_g the capital gains rate.[7] If corporations completely replaced dividend payments with stock repurchases as a matter of policy, the factor in the numerator of this expression would become $(1 - t_g)$ instead and we would have

$$R_R = \alpha_t \frac{(1 - t_g)}{(1 - t_g)} = \alpha_t. \tag{8-1}$$

Retained earnings would, in effect, become a more expensive source of capital because the after-tax value of the relevant alternative—cash payments to shareholders—would increase. A decision by the firm to reinvest would require shareholders to forego more after-tax income than was specified in our original analysis and consequently make it necessary for the investments undertaken out of retentions to earn at a higher rate in order to be justified. Until stock repurchases do substantially eliminate the payment of dividends, however, that earlier model remains valid.[8]

STOCK DIVIDENDS AND SPLITS

A related question has to do with the impact on share prices of stock splits and stock dividends. Is it possible for a firm to increase its total market value simply by changing the number of shares it has outstanding? Logic—and the weight of current scholarly opinion—would suggest a negative reply. Given the firm's investments, the level of its borrowing, and therefore its aggregate after-interest-and-tax profit prospects, it should make no difference how many pieces of paper it happens to hand out to its owners. The product

$$V_S = \text{(price per share)} \times \text{(number of shares)}$$

should be a constant. Two shares of stock promising $5 a year should not sell for more in total than one share promising $10. The same argument—in reverse—is the basis for the stock repurchase discussion above. If a corporation uses its redundant cash to remove some of its shares from the market and retire them, the price of those

[7] As discussed on pp. 67–68.

[8] A simple adjustment in equation (5–45) which would recognize the opportunity firms have to utilize stock repurchases as at least part of their overall strategy would be to assume t_p to be slightly less than twice t_g on average. For a more extensive and rigorous discussion of the stock repurchase decision, see Edwin J. Elton and Martin J. Gruber, "The Effect of Share Repurchases on the Value of the Firm," *Journal of Finance*, March 1968, pp. 135–149.

remaining should rise correspondingly to reflect higher per-share future income prospects.

Why, then, do firms occasionally split their stock and pay stock dividends—and why does it often seem that the share prices involved do not fall quite in proportion? Thus, it is not unusual to see a $60 stock which is split two-for-one end up selling for more than $30 afterward. One answer commonly given is that, by lowering the shares' price range, the market for them is broadened to include more small investors. People who will not consider a $60 stock because it is "high-priced" will buy it if it trades near $30 instead. They will be attracted to the opportunity to buy what in market terminology is called a "round lot"—100 shares—for $3,000, whereas they would not think of buying 50 shares at $60. If this sounds a little bizarre, there does seem to be some truth in it. A possible reason is that the brokerage commissions on a round lot are smaller per share so that there *is* a slight saving on such purchases as compared with "odd lots" of less than 100 shares. Since this saving is fairly small, however, the main factor seems to be purely psychological. Enough people appear to like lower-priced shares that the firm does get some benefit out of keeping the trading range of its stock at an appropriate level through periodic splits.[9]

A more rational sort of explanation for the same phenomenon involves the effect of stock splits on investors' expectations. The market may interpret the act of splitting in itself as an indication that the firm's subsequent earnings and dividends are likely to be higher than were previously anticipated. The firm in a sense is telling the world that the time has come to bring its share price down to a more manageable level because it looks as though even further increases will soon be forthcoming. This alerts investors to the company's bright future and—if the brightness is in fact there and has just not been fully appreciated before—a price increase is a logical result. In that respect, a stock split may be said to contain implicitly some useful information about management's confidence in the firm's prospects.

---

[9] On the other hand, there seems to be a feeling that it is possible to err on the low side as well. Several years ago, the Studebaker Corporation *combined* its stock in the ratio 1:5 in order to raise the relevant price from approximately $7 per share to $35. The concern was that a $7 figure made the company look too "cheap"—i.e., speculative and probably a little disreputable—and thereby discouraged respectable investors from being interested in its shares.

An even more concrete way of expressing that confidence, of course, is to raise the company's cash dividend simultaneously. This seems the most likely justification for any hopes that a corporation's total market value will increase, particularly in the case of a stock dividend. If a firm "pays" a 5 percent stock dividend—giving its shareholders one additional piece of paper for every 20 they now own —but does not adjust its per-share cash dividend payment downward by the same fraction, the effect is to augment its owners' aggregate annual cash income by 5 percent. It would therefore come as no surprise if it turned out that the per-share price of the company's stock held steady. The basis for such a result, however, is the behavior of the relevant cash payments rather than the presence of extra stock certificates. The firm could achieve the same objective by skipping the latter entirely and simply raising its per-share cash payout.

As an illustration, consider the situation of a company which has been paying $5 per share cash dividend every year for many years. Its earnings have fluctuated, but have exhibited no tendency to grow over time and there is no expectation of higher dividends to come. Its current stock price is $50. Suddenly, one of its products catches on with consumers and it becomes clear that earnings will jump to a new level that will permit dividends to be raised to—and maintained at—$5.25 a share. If the firm increases its payout in that manner, a new stock price of $52.50 can be anticipated. If instead it issues a 5 percent stock dividend and keeps the cash payment at $5.00, the price should continue to be $50. Either way, every original shareholder will own stock worth a total of $52.50, will be receiving $5.25 annually in cash dividends, and will eventually have to pay tax on a $2.50 capital gain. But the cause of these happy circumstances is the improvement in the firm's profit position and thereby in its ability to generate income for its owners—not an increase in the number of pieces of paper those individuals have in their safety deposit boxes.[10]

By way of comic relief, the following news item from the December 20, 1965, *Wall Street Journal* suggests the confusion which often attends discussions of the efficacy of stock dividends. As a charitable gesture, the company and the executive involved will be allowed to remain anonymous:

[10] For a more extensive discussion, see C. A. Barker, "Effective Stock Splits," *Harvard Business Review,* January–February 1956, pp. 101–106, and "Evaluation of Stock Dividends," *Harvard Business Review,* July–August 1958, pp. 99–114.

The XXX Corporation today declared a 2.5 percent stock dividend payable February 1 to stock of record January 3. It is the first dividend declared by the company since it was formed in 1945. John Doe, Senior Vice-President for Finance, said: "This has been a very good financial year and we felt we should recognize this by a stock dividend to our shareholders. Because of our equipment program, we felt we shouldn't pay it in cash."

Wouldn't a 5 percent dividend have been twice as good?

PREFERRED STOCK

One source of corporate capital which was not discussed in the preceding chapters—largely because it has fallen into disuse in recent years—is preferred stock. Whereas in the 1920s preferred comprised approximately 11 percent of American corporations' total long-term capitalization, this figure had declined to about 4 percent by the mid-1950s and was still falling.[11] Most firms today borrow rather than issue preferred stock when they feel a "senior" security is called for in their capital structure. The argument usually runs that preferred stock has all the disadvantages of debt (i.e., an annual obligation which must be met before dividends on common stock can be paid) and none of the advantages (preferred dividends are not tax deductible as interest charges are). While, as we shall see, this is too simple a characterization of the situation, the resulting conclusion that preferred stock should be used only infrequently *is* legitimate.

Let us return to our familiar comparison between firms A and B in the same risk class. The assumption again is that both are entirely common-stock-financed to begin with and that both have in prospect an aggregate annual pre-tax earnings stream described by a mean $\bar{Y}$ and a variance $\sigma^2(Y)$. With the same number of common shares outstanding, N, the per-share market price in both cases will be

$$P_t = \frac{\bar{Y}(1 - t_c)/N}{\alpha_t},\qquad(8\text{--}2)$$

assuming that all earnings are paid out as dividends each year. The mean of per-share earnings and dividends is $\bar{Y}(1 - t_c)/N$ and the variance $(1 - t_c)^2\sigma^2(Y)/N^2$. The total market value of each firm comes to just

---

[11] Merton H. Miller, "The Corporation Income Tax and Corporate Financial Policies," *Stabilization Policies,* Commission on Money and Credit Supporting Papers (Englewood Cliffs, N.J.: Prentice-Hall, Inc., 1963).

$$V_t = NP_t. \qquad (8\text{--}3)$$

Suppose, then, that firm A decides to issue preferred stock in the amount V_P and to retire the fraction V_P/V_t of its common shares with the proceeds. This will leave

$$N\left(1 - \frac{V_P}{V_t}\right) \qquad (8\text{--}4)$$

such shares still on the market and will produce an annual dividend stream *after* preferred dividends and taxes for each of them equal to

$$y_A = \frac{Y(1 - t_c) - cV_P}{N\left(1 - \dfrac{V_P}{V_t}\right)}, \qquad (8\text{--}5)$$

where c denotes the "coupon" dividend rate on the preferred. Thus, if preferred stock is issued in denominations of $100 and the annual dividend promised is $5, c becomes .05 for purposes of this equation. Since preferred dividends are not tax deductible, the corporate tax t_c is assessed against the firm's total income Y before cV_P is subtracted. The common stockholders must, in effect, make good the preferred dividend commitment without any help from the government.[12] The mean and variance of per-common-share annual earnings and dividends for firm A therefore are

$$\bar{y}_A = \frac{\bar{Y}(1 - t_c) - cV_P}{N\left(1 - \dfrac{V_P}{V_t}\right)} \qquad (8\text{--}6)$$

$$\sigma^2(y_A) = \frac{(1 - t_c)^2 \sigma^2(Y)}{N^2\left(1 - \dfrac{V_P}{V_t}\right)^2}, \qquad (8\text{--}7)$$

and the question is whether an income stream with these features should sell for a price other than P_t.

In order to show that it should not, we must adopt a slightly different approach than in the case of our previous debt-equity analysis. An individual investor cannot issue his own preferred stock and spend the money on common shares in the same way he could "issue" personal debt—i.e., borrow—to purchase equities. What he *can* do, however, is use a portion of his funds to acquire the common stock of firm A and invest the remainder in its preferred stock, thereby putting

---

[12] For a comparison with the leverage discussion, see equation (4–3).

himself in a position equivalent to a shareholder in firm B which has no preferred outstanding.

Consider the following strategy: an individual sets aside the amount

$$P_t + P_t \frac{V_P}{(V_t - V_p)} = \frac{P_t}{\left(1 - \frac{V_P}{V_t}\right)} \tag{8-8}$$

of his personal capital for investment in firms belonging to the risk class we are examining.[13] If he uses those funds to buy into firm B, he can acquire a total of

$$\frac{1}{1 - \frac{V_p}{V_t}} \tag{8-9}$$

shares at P_t dollars apiece. This action will provide him with an income stream having the characteristics

$$\bar{y}_B = \frac{\bar{Y}(1 - t_c)}{N\left(1 - \frac{V_P}{V_t}\right)} \tag{8-10}$$

$$\sigma^2(y)_B = \frac{(1 - t_c)^2 \sigma^2(Y)}{N^2 \left(1 - \frac{V_P}{V_t}\right)^2}, \tag{8-11}$$

since *one* share in firm B offers a mean of $\bar{Y}(1 - t_c)/N$ and a variance of $(1 - t_c)^2 \sigma^2(Y)/N^2$. If instead our man spends

$$\frac{P_t V_P}{V_t - V_P} \tag{8-12}$$

dollars of his funds on the preferred stock of firm A, he will lay claim to a guaranteed annual income equal to

$$\frac{c P_t V_P}{V_t - V_P}. \tag{8-13}$$

That is, for every dollar so invested, the company will pay him c dollars a year in return. If, then, firm A's common stock is still selling for P_t dollars per share, the investor can buy precisely one share with the money he will have left. That share will add the probabilistic

---

[13] This figure is quite arbitrary and is chosen only because it makes the relevant comparisons convenient. It could be scaled upward or downward at will without changing our conclusions.

income stream y_A described above to his preferred dividends and give him an aggregate set of prospects expressable as

$$y_T = y_A + \frac{cP_tV_P}{V_t - V_P} \tag{8-14}$$

$$y_T = \frac{Y(1 - t_c) - cV_P}{N\left(1 - \frac{V_P}{V_t}\right)} + \frac{cP_tV_P}{V_t\left(1 - \frac{V_P}{V_t}\right)}, \tag{8-15}$$

but we know that $P_t = V_t/N$. Thus

$$y_T = \frac{Y(1 - t_c) - cV_P}{N\left(1 - \frac{V_P}{V_t}\right)} + \frac{cV_P}{N\left(1 - \frac{V_P}{V_t}\right)}, \tag{8-16}$$

or simply,

$$y_T = \frac{Y(1 - t_c)}{N\left(1 - \frac{V_P}{V_t}\right)}, \tag{8-17}$$

and this income stream has a mean and variance of

$$\bar{y}_T = \frac{\bar{Y}(1 - t_c)}{N\left(1 - \frac{V_P}{V_t}\right)} \tag{8-18}$$

$$\sigma^2(y_T) = \frac{(1 - t_c)^2\sigma^2(Y)}{N^2\left(1 - \frac{V_P}{V_t}\right)^2}, \tag{8-19}$$

which exactly match the parameters of the income stream y_B. The condition that the per-share price of firm A's common stock continue to be P_t must therefore hold, since no investor will pay any more than that amount as long as the common stock of firm B and the preferred of firm A are available. In consequence, the presence of preferred stock in a corporation's capital structure should have no effect on the market price of its common. The complementary proposition—which should not require a proof at this stage in our discussion —is that the costs of capital for preferred and common stock are identical. An investment financed either way must produce the same rate of return if the firm's shareholders are to be as well off as if the investment were not made and the funds not raised.[14]

---

[14] Actually, since in theory the cost of both common and preferred turn out to be equal to the market capitalization rate α_t, it is likely as a practical matter

To illustrate the argument, consider two all-common-stock-financed firms whose probability distributions of future annual pre-tax earnings both have the form:

Possible Y	Probability
$2.2 million	$\frac{1}{3}$
2.0 million	$\frac{1}{3}$
1.8 million	$\frac{1}{3}$

If each has 100,000 shares outstanding and both pay out all their earnings as dividends, the *after-tax* per-share annual dividend outcomes are:

Possible y	Probability
$11	$\frac{1}{3}$
10	$\frac{1}{3}$
9	$\frac{1}{3}$

and, assuming a $100 per share market price, we have

$$\alpha_t = \frac{\bar{Y}(1 - t_c)/N}{P_t} = \frac{\$10}{\$100} = .10. \qquad (8\text{--}20)$$

Firm A now issues 50,000 shares of $100 preferred stock carrying a $5 annual dividend obligation. With the $5 million thus obtained, it retires one-half its common stock. The annual prospects for the 50,000 remaining shares are therefore:

Possible $Y(1 - t_c)$	Less: Preferred Dividends of $250,000	Per Common Share	Probability
$1,100,000	$850,000	$17	$\frac{1}{3}$
1,000,000	750,000	15	$\frac{1}{3}$
900,000	650,000	13	$\frac{1}{3}$

If an individual investor takes $100 and buys one of firm A's *preferred* shares, he can anticipate a steady annual income of $5. How

---

that preferred will be slightly the "cheaper" of the two. When we take underwriting expenses and underpricing into account, the gap between the prevailing market price and the net proceeds realized from a new issue will almost certainly be greater for common stock. Denoting the two percentage gaps as b_E and b_P, we have

$$R_E = \frac{\alpha_t}{1 - b_E} > R_P = \frac{\alpha_t}{1 - b_P}$$

as the required rates of return, where $b_E > b_P$ in almost every actual situation.

much, then, will he be willing to pay for one of the company's *common* shares, given that such an acquisition would bring his total annual income possibilities to:

Preferred Dividend	Common Dividend	Total	Probability
$5	$17	$22	$\frac{1}{3}$
5	15	20	$\frac{1}{3}$
5	13	18	$\frac{1}{3}$

The answer must be just $100, because as an alternative he could simply take his $200, buy two shares of firm B common, and get this *same* set of outcomes. Thus, the "leverage" in earnings and dividends created by preferred stock is of no real value to a corporation's common stockholders. They can duplicate the results of the firm's actions in their own portfolios.

Intuitively, this conclusion should come as no surprise. We saw earlier that the only reason corporate borrowing was a good idea was the tax deductibility of interest charges. Since that advantage is not present in connection with preferred stock dividends, we return in effect to the equivalent of the no-tax debt analysis of Chapter 3. The irrelevance of a firm's debt-equity ratio in that world is matched here by the irrelevance of its preferred-to-common ratio.

All this does leave a question unsettled, however. If common stockholders neither gain nor lose if preferred stock rather than additional common is issued when the company needs external equity capital for expansion, why isn't preferred stock used more often? The law of averages would suggest that the two sources would be relied on to about the same extent in practice if the discussion above were correct. In fact, if the underwriting-and-underpricing gap for new issues is apt to be smaller for preferred, we ought to observe quite a lot of such securities being sold each year.

The reason why we don't is simple. The analysis presented—like that for debt—is valid only so long as the firm stays within its ability to satisfy creditors and preferred shareholders that the promises made to them can be kept. Thus, the phenomenon which was referred to previously as a corporation's "debt limit" should more appropriately be thought of as its "senior security limit." The firm can commit itself to pay only up to a certain total amount of preferred dividends and interest every year and still attract lenders and preferred shareholders. Beyond that point, no additional senior capital of either type will be forthcoming—and our conclusions that debt is advantageous and preferred is immaterial will no longer hold. Even if the company could thereafter induce some institution to lend it a little more money, the stock market would react adversely to the increased risk exposure of the common stockholders, and share prices would fall.

The implication, of course, is that if there is a limit of this kind, and if debt is a better financing method than preferred stock up to that limit, the latter will always get "squeezed out" of the capital structure. Firms will always borrow rather than issue *either* preferred or common stock as long as they can—and when they can't any more because the indicated limit has been reached, the possibility of using preferred also disappears. Indeed, since interest charges are tax deductible, the "senior security limit" is effectively higher for a firm which borrows than for one which employs preferred stock. At a 50 percent corporate tax rate, a firm can support twice as much in the way of annual interest payments as it can preferred dividends. Moreover, if the interest rate involved is the same as the preferred dividend rate, twice the dollar amount of debt can be obtained by the firm before it exhausts its ability to attract such capital from investors.

Now, the foregoing is somewhat overstated. The promises a corporation makes to its preferred shareholders are more flexible than those made to creditors in that preferred dividends can be missed for a few years without the firm's being forced into bankruptcy or reorganization. If interest payments cannot be met in a given year, however, the firm is in real trouble. Its common stockholders are therefore better protected from the more severe consequences of a temporary decline in earnings when preferred is issued. This suggests that the senior security limit can be stretched to a certain extent for such financing and that a small slice of preferred can probably be inserted into the firm's capital structure at the top of its debt capacity. But it should be recalled that the only benefit obtained by the common stockholders from this policy is that small difference between the flotation costs of common and preferred noted above. Otherwise, additional common stock might just as well be sold. The current unpopularity of preferred which our empirical evidence documents makes it appear as though this advantage is, in fact, not considered very significant by corporate management.[15]

In any case, the weighted average cost of capital for a firm which does have some preferred on its balance sheet can readily be expressed as

---

[15] Miller, *op. cit.*

$$R_A = X_E R_E + X_D R_D + X_R R_R + X_P R_P, \tag{8-21}$$

where X_P refers to the fraction of total long-term capital supplied by preferred stock issues and, as specified,

$$R_P = \frac{\alpha_t}{1 - b_P} \tag{8-22}$$

for the cost of the preferred. The other items in equation (8-21) are those defined earlier, the condition now being that

$$X_E + X_D + X_R + X_P = 1. \tag{8-23}$$

The various fractions of total capitalization represented by common stock, debt, retained earnings, and preferred must always add to unity.

DEPRECIATION

Another source of long-term funds, about which little is said explicitly in most discussions of capital structure, is the corporation's depreciation charges. To the extent that these are reinvested in new plant and equipment, what impact do they have on our cost of capital prescriptions?

In reality, of course, depreciation is not a "source" of funds. Rather, the firm's selling operations are the source, but the reported after-tax profit from those operations understates their contribution to funds flow to the extend of the noncash expenses charged against income—depreciation typically being the most significant such charge. Whatever the interpretation, the funds *are* there to be used and the question of their "cost" must be confronted.

If we think of the implications of *not* reinvesting those funds in the firm, the answer to that question becomes clear. Given a target capital structure for the firm—that is, a specified combination of debt, retained earnings, and common stock issues to be used in raising capital—how logically would depreciation cash flows that were not to be reinvested be distributed to the corporation's securityholders? Clearly, in the same proportions that external funds were raised in the first place, in order to maintain the target capital structure intact. Thus, the appropriate strategy would be to repay some debt, pay some dividends, and repurchase some common shares in exactly the proportions X_D,

X_R, and X_E. From that perspective, a decision not to reinvest depreciation flows represents a cash-payout decision which is simply the mirror image of a decision to raise net new capital. Accordingly, the cost of reinvesting those flows is precisely the same as the cost of raising new funds: the R_A we have identified in our analysis above. Once that figure is computed for the firm's target capital structure, we know all we need to know about the "cost of capital" for depreciation reinvestment. Another way to make the point is to think of the availability of depreciation cash flows as diminishing the net fund-raising burden of the firm—and that burden will be shared by debt, retentions, and stock issues according to the long-term policies of the enterprise. By either view, the cost of reinvested depreciation is just the R_A we have derived, and no additional computations are necessary.

CHANGES IN INTEREST RATES

An additional matter we have only touched upon in our discussions thus far is that of the effect on the corporation's common stockholders of changes in the going market rate of interest on borrowings. We noted in Chapter 4 that, in the basic measurement equation

$$K = \alpha_t + (\alpha_t - r)(1 - t_C)(D/V_S), \qquad (4\text{-}45)$$

the values to be inserted for r, D, and V_S should be the prevailing market magnitudes and that, in particular, if interest rates had changed since the firm involved originally issued its debt, the appropriate figure for D would not be the stated book value of that debt. We did not, however, identify the associated consequences for shareholders, in terms of the impact on the price of the company's stock. That effort is of some relevance, since it leads us directly to a bond refunding decision rule.[16]

Consider the circumstances of the owners of a corporation whose outstanding bonds carry a coupon rate of interest equal to the prevailing market rate r_M. If those bonds are consols—

---

[16]The material in this section is taken in part from an article entitled "Some Extensions of Capital Structure Theory," which appeared in the January, 1975, issue of the *Journal of Business Research*. The author acknowledges the journal's permission to excerpt from that analysis.

i.e., have no maturity and promise a payment to bondholders of size $r_M D$ annually—the total market value of the firm will be, from equation (4-21):

$$V_L = \frac{\overline{Y}(1 - t_C)}{\alpha_t} + \frac{r_M D t_C}{r_M}$$

or

$$V_L = V_U + D t_C \qquad (8\text{-}24)$$

where V_L represents the sum of the market values of the firm's common shares, V_S, plus its debt, V_D. If the coupon rate on the debt is the same as the going market rate, of course, the debt will sell at par, and $V_D = D$. Thus,

$$V_S = V_U - (1 - t_C)D. \qquad (8\text{-}25)$$

On the other hand, if the coupon on the bonds at the time they were issued was some rate r_C different from today's r_M, we would have

$$V_L = V_U + \frac{r_C D t_C}{r_m} \qquad (8\text{-}26)$$

and the market value of the debt would be

$$V_D = \frac{r_C D}{r_m} \qquad (8\text{-}27)$$

whereupon the market value of the firm's common stock would become

$$V_S{}' = V_U - (1 - t_C)(D)\left(\frac{r_C}{r_M}\right) \qquad (8\text{-}28)$$

and the difference in shareholder wealth positions in the two situations can be identified by subtracting equation (8-25) from equation (8-28), as

$$V_S{}' - V_S = (1 - t_C)(D)\left(1 - \frac{r_C}{r_M}\right). \qquad (8\text{-}29)$$

Accordingly, if interest rates rise subsequent to a bond issue $(r_M > r_C)$, shareholders benefit by having old, low-rate debt in the firm's capital structure; if rates fall, they are penalized. Equation (8-29) specifies the magnitude of the gain or loss. As an illustration, a company whose management was clever enough to have borrowed $20 million at a time when only a 6 percent coupon rate was required to sell the bonds will have provided shareholders with a share price "windfall" gain, if rates later rise to 8 percent, amounting to

$$V_S' - V_S = (1 - .5)(\$20)\left(1 - \frac{.06}{.08}\right) \qquad (8\text{-}30)$$

or a total of $2.5 million, assuming a 50 percent corporate tax rate.

FINITE-MATURITY BORROWINGS

Our analysis, however, need not be confined to the admittedly peculiar case of consol (perpetual) bond issues. If the firm's debt obligations have a maturity date N years in the future, the counterpart of equation (4-21) simply becomes

$$V_L = \frac{Y(1 - t_C)}{\alpha_t} + \sum_{t=1}^{N} \frac{r_M D t_C}{(1 + r_M)^t} \qquad (8\text{-}31)$$

wherein the summation expressed in the second term on the right-hand side of the equation now runs only to year N rather than to infinity, as it did for consol bonds. To simplify the expression, let

$$A_N = \sum_{t=1}^{N} \frac{1}{(1 + r_M)^t} \qquad (8\text{-}32)$$

where, in effect, A_N denotes the present value of an N-year annuity of one dollar, discounted at the rate r_M. Thus,

$$V_L = V_S + V_D = V_U + r_M D t_C A_N. \qquad (8\text{-}33)$$

Now, the market value of the bonds, V_D, will be the present value to investors of the cash flows they expect to get from owning them. Given that they require a yield of r_M, then,

$$V_D = \sum_{t=1}^{N} \frac{r_M D}{(1 + r_M)^t} + \frac{D}{(1 + r_M)^N} \qquad (8\text{-}34)$$

which is the standard present value formula for a series of N-year cash flows of size $r_M D$ (the interest payments) and a final principal repayment of size D. Letting

$$P_N = 1/(1 + r_M)^N, \qquad (8\text{-}35)$$

we have

$$V_D = r_M D A_N + D P_N \qquad (8\text{-}36)$$

and therefore

$$V_S = V_U + r_M D t_C A_N - r_M D A_N - D P_N \qquad (8\text{-}37)$$

If instead, the bonds carried a coupon rate r_C, the total market value of the corporation would be

$$V_L = V_S' + V_D' = V_U + r_C D t_C A_N \qquad (8\text{-}38)$$

and

$$V_D' = r_C D A_N + D P_N \qquad (8\text{-}39)$$

which implies that

$$V_S' = V_U + r_C D t_C A_N - r_C D A_N - D P_N \qquad (8\text{-}40)$$

and the difference in shareholder wealth positions can once more be identified by subtracting (8-37) from (8-40). The result is

$$V_S' - V_S = (1 - t_C)(D A_N)(r_M - r_C) \qquad (8\text{-}41)$$

and the implication is similar to that derived for perpetual debt issues: if interest rates rise, shareholders gain; if they fall, shareholders lose. Equation (8-41) tells us how much.

BOND REFUNDING

That expression, then, is the basis for developing a bond refunding decision rule. The disadvantage to shareholders of having imbedded, high-rate (r_C) debt in the firm's capital structure when prevailing rates have diminished to r_M is measured precisely by the difference $V_S' - V_S$ shown above, since a one-for-one substitution of bonds in the amount D at the new, lower rate for their high-rate predecessors would just wipe out that difference. Given this index of potential refunding benefit, therefore, the relevant managerial question is simply one of identifying the transactions costs to the firm of engaging in the substitution. These consist of: (1) the call premium, if any, on the old bonds; (2) the legal and underwriting fees which must be paid for retirement of the old, and registration and issue of the new, obligations; (3) whatever dual interest payments are occasioned by the inevitable period of overlap between the sale of the new bonds and the extinction of the old ones. All of these constitute actual cash outlays required of the firm as part of the refunding process, and all must be borne directly by shareholders. Fortunately, they are also all tax-deductible in the year of the transaction. If we denote their total by T, the desirability of the refunding opportunity is thereby fully specified by the comparison

$$-T(1 - t_C) \gtreqless (1 - t_C)(r_M - r_C)(DA_N) \quad (8\text{-}42)$$

where the expression on the left-hand side represents the cost to stockholders of refunding, and that on the right the cost of *not* refunding. More succinctly, the test is:

$$T \lesseqgtr (r_C - r_M)(DA_N) \quad (8\text{-}43)$$

and the corporate tax rate can be eliminated from consideration. Accordingly, if the present value of the annual difference between the old and new total pre-tax annual interest payments on the borrowings involved, capitalized over the period of the maturity of the existing bond issue at the rate r_M prevailing in the market, is greater than the cash transactions costs associated with refunding, the bonds *should* be replaced.

This decision criterion—which has a degree of intuitive appeal—bears some general resemblance to portions of various recommendations made previously in the literature.[17] It is, however, the only one anchored in a systematic treatment of underlying levered-firm security valuation patterns which addresses the matter of finite maturities explicitly. It has, for that reason, the additional virtue of supplying unambiguous

---

[17] H. Bierman, "The Bond Refunding Decision," *Financial Management*, Summer 1972; O.D. Bowlin, "The Refunding Decision: Another Special Case in Capital Budgeting," *Journal of Finance*, March 1966; E. Schwartz, "The Refunding Decision," *Journal of Business*, October 1967.

answers to certain questions attendant upon refunding which have been subjects of contention. For one thing, it is evident from our derivation that the appropriate discount rate to use in valuing prospective interest savings is in fact the current *before*-tax market rate r_M demanded by lenders (as contained in A_N), not that rate's post-corporate-tax counterpart and not an equity or some weighted-average-cost-of-capital rate. The valuation processes at issue permit no other conclusion.

Further, it is equally clear that the correct horizon for the appraisal *is* precisely the term to maturity of the old bonds. A decision by management to lengthen maturities while refunding is a separate decision, whose impact on shareholders should not be attributed to the refunding itself. It is necessary, therefore, to disentangle this phenomenon from the "pure" refunding operation, as we have in equation (8-43). That stipulation also emerges directly from the basic market mechanisms portrayed.

SUMMARY

While a wide range of additional topics might be examined, the major elements in the firm's decision about the form of its long-term financing have been covered and we have pretty well reached the point of diminishing returns. The more the cost of capital question is expanded from here on in, the more we shall begin to encroach on matters that are better treated elsewhere. For that reason, a few summary comments are all that remain to be offered.

Perhaps the most important element in the analysis is the proposition that an improvement in the economic well-being of a corporation's owners—its common stockholders—should be the goal of all its financial policies. Since that well-being can be measured very conveniently and very directly by the market value of the firm's shares, the conclusion is that an increase in the price of the latter should be management's basic objective and the criterion by which the efficacy of its decisions are judged. In operational terms, this means that the process of calculating and minimizing a firm's cost of capital is precisely the process we call "security valuation." The concern of our discussion therefore has been to predict the effect on stock prices of alternative financing strategies, taking into account throughout the opportunities which exist for individual investors to arrange their own portfolios so as to achieve many of the same results. Only if a corporation can do something by adjusting its capital structure that its shareholders cannot do for themselves does it seem logical to believe the market will "pay" the firm—via an increased stock price—to make such an adjustment. The argument has been that, by this standard, the only real differences between the desirability of the various sources of long-term corporate funds are created by the federal income tax. Given the nature of that tax, however, a hierarchy of capital costs can be established and some guidelines for reducing the weighted average figure for the firm developed. While it cannot be pretended here that all—or even most—of the problems raised in this connection have been put to rest, the hope is that at least some understanding of the major issues has been provided.

BIBLIOGRAPHY

Alchian, Armen A. "The Meaning of Utility Measurement." *American Economic Review*, March 1953.

Ang, J. "Weighted Average vs. True Cost of Capital." *Financial Management*, Autumn 1973.

Arditti, F. "The Weighted Average Cost of Capital: Some Questions on its Definition, Interpretation, and Use." *Journal of Finance*, September 1973.

Barges, Alexander. *The Effect of Capital Structure on the Cost of Capital.* Englewood Cliffs, N.J.: Prentice-Hall, Inc., 1963.

Barker, C. Austin. "Effective Stock Splits." *Harvard Business Review*, January-February 1956.

———. "Evaluation of Stock Dividends." *Harvard Business Review*, July-August 1958.

Bierman, H. "The Bond Refunding Decision." *Financial Management*, Summer 1972.

Bodenhorn, Diran. "On the Problem of Capital Budgeting." *Journal of Finance*, December 1959.

Bowlin, O.D. "The Refunding Decision: Another Special Case in Capital Budgeting." *Journal of Finance*, March 1966.

Brennan, M.J. "Taxes, Market Valuation, and Corporate Financial Policy." *National Tax Journal*, December 1970.

Donaldson, Gordon. "New Framework for Corporate Debt Policy." *Harvard Business Review*, March-April 1962.

Durand, David. "The Cost of Debt and Equity Funds for Business: Trends and Problems of Measurement." In *Conference on Research in Business Finance.* New York: National Bureau of Economic Research, 1952.

———. "Growth Stocks and the Petersburg Paradox." *The Journal of Finance*, September 1957.

Ellis, D.C. "Repurchase Stock to Revitalize Equity." *Harvard Business Review*, July-August 1965.

Elton, Edwin J., and Gruber, Martin J. "The Effect of Share Repurchases on the Value of the Firm." *Journal of Finance*, March 1968.

———. "Marginal Stockholder Tax Rates and the Clientele Effect." *Review of Economics and Statistics*, February 1970.

Farrar, D.E., and Selwyn, L.L. "Taxes, Corporate Financial Policies, and Returns to Investors." *National Tax Journal* December 1967.

Friedman, Milton, and Savage, Leonard J. "The Utility Analysis of Choices Involving Risk." *Journal of Political Economy*, August 1948.

Gordon, Myron J. *The Investment, Financing, and Valuation of the Corporation*. Homewood, Ill.: Richard D. Irwin, Inc., 1962.

Gordon, Myron J., and Shapiro, Eli. "Capital Equipment Analysis: The Required Rate of Profit." *Management Science*, October 1956.

Guthart, L.A. "More Companies Are Buying Back Their Own Stock." *Harvard Business Review*, March-April 1965.

Haley, C.W. "Taxes, the Cost of Capital, and the Firm's Investment Decisions." *Journal of Finance*, September 1971.

Haley, C., and Schall, L. *The Theory of Financial Decisions*. New York: McGraw-Hill, 1973.

Hamada, R.S. "The Effect of the Firm's Capital Structure on the Systematic Risk of Common Stocks." *Journal of Finance*, May 1972.

———. "Portfolio Analysis, Market Equilibrium, and Corporate Finance." *Journal of Finance*, March 1969.

Haugen, R.A., and Pappas, J.L. "Equilibrium in the Pricing of Capital Assets, Risk-Bearing Debt Instruments, and the Question of Optimal Capital Structure." *Journal of Financial and Quantitative Analysis*, June 1971.

Hirshleifer, J. *Investment, Interest, and Capital*. Englewood Cliffs, N.J.: Prentice-Hall, Inc., 1970.

Lewellen, Wilbur G. "A Conceptual Re-Appraisal of Cost of Capital." *Financial Management*, Winter 1974.

———. *Executive Compensation in Large Industrial Corporations*. New York: National Bureau of Economic Research, 1968.

———. "Managerial Pay and the Tax Changes of the 1960s." *National Tax Journal*, June 1972.

———. "Some Extensions of Capital Structure Theory." *Journal of Business Research*, January 1975.

Lewellen, Wilbur G., and Racette, G. "Convertible Debt Financing." *Journal of Financial and Quantitative Analysis*, December 1973.

Linke C., and Kim, M. "More on the Weighted Average Cost of Capital: A Comment and Analysis." *Journal of Financial and Quantitative Analysis*, December 1974.

Lintner, J. "The Valuation of Risk Assets and the Selection of Risky Investments in Stock Portfolios and Capital Budgets." *Review of Economics and Statistics*, February 1965.

Lintner, John. "Distribution of Incomes of Corporations between Dividends, Retained Earnings, and Taxes." *American Economic Review*, May 1956.

———. "Dividends, Earnings, Leverage, Stock Prices, and the Supply of Capital to Corporations." *Review of Economics and Statistics*, August 1962.

Luce, R.D., and Raiffa, Howard. *Games and Decisions*. New York: John Wiley & Sons, Inc., 1957.

Markowitz, Harry. "Portfolio Selection." *Journal of Finance*, March 1952.

Miller, Merton H. "The Corporation Income Tax and Corporate Financial Policies." *Stabilization Policies*, Commission on Money and Credit Supporting Papers. Englewood Cliffs, N.J.: Prentice-Hall, Inc., 1963.

Miller, Merton H., and Modigliani, Franco. "Dividend Policy, Growth, and the Valuation of Shares." *Journal of Business*, October 1961.

Modigliani, Franco, and Miller, Merton H. "Corporate Income Taxes and the Cost of Capital: A Correction." *American Economic Review*, June 1963.

———. "The Cost of Capital, Corporation Finance, and the Theory of Investment." *American Economic Review*, June 1958.

Mossin, J. "Security Pricing and Investment Criteria in Competitive Markets." *American Economic Review*, December 1969.

———. *Theory of Financial Markets*. Englewood Cliffs, N.J.: Prentice-Hall, 1973.

Myers, S. "Interactions of Corporate Financing and Investment Decisions—Implications for Capital Budgeting." *Journal of Finance*, March 1974.

Reilly, R., and Wecker, W. "On the Weighted Average Cost of Capital." *Journal of Financial and Quantitative Analysis*, January 1973.

Robichek, Alexander A., and Myers, Stewart C. *Optimal Financing Decisions*. Englewood Cliffs, N.J.: Prentice-Hall, Inc., 1965.

———. "Problems in the Theory of Optimal Capital Structure." *Journal of Financial and Quantitative Analysis*, June 1966.

Robinson, Roland I. *Financing the Dynamic Small Firm*. Belmont, Calif.: Wadsworth Publishing Company, Inc., 1966.

Rubinstein, M.E. "A Mean-Variance Synthesis of Corporate Financial Theory." *Journal of Finance*, March 1973.

Schall, L.D. "Asset Valuation, Firm Investment, and Firm Diversification." *Journal of Business*, January 1972.

Schwartz, E. "The Refunding Decision." *Journal of Business*, October 1967.

Sharpe, William F. "Capital Asset Prices: A Theory of Market Equilibrium Under Conditions of Risk." *Journal of Finance*, September 1964.

———. "A Simplified Model for Portfolio Analysis." *Management Science*, January 1963.

Sharpe, William W. *Portfolio Theory and Capital Markets*. New York: McGraw-Hill, 1970.

Solomon, Ezra. "Leverage and the Cost of Capital." *Journal of Finance*, May 1963.

———. *The Management of Corporate Capital*. New York: The Free Press, 1959.

———. *The Theory of Financial Management*. New York: Columbia University Press, 1963.

Stapleton, R.C. "Taxes, the Cost of Capital, and the Theory of Investment." *Economic Journal*, December 1972.

Stiglitz, J. "On the Irrelevance of Corporate Financial Policy." *American Economic Review*, December 1974.

———. "A Re-Examination of the Modigliani-Miller Theorem." *American Economic Review*, December 1969.

Walter, James E. *Dividend Policy and Enterprise Valuation*. Belmont, Calif.: Wadsworth Publishing Company, Inc., 1967.

———. "Dividend Policy: Its Influence on the Value of the Enterprise." *Journal of Finance*, May 1963.

"Weighted Average vs. True Cost of Capital: Reilly, Brigham, Linke and Kim versus Ang." *Financial Management*, Spring 1974.